P9-CCR-342

Better Homes and Gardens®
SALADS

BETTER HOMES AND GARDENS® BOOKS
Des Moines

SALADS
Editors: Linda Henry, Mary Major Williams
Graphic Designer: Michael Burns
Project Manager: Jennifer Speer Ramundt

Associate Department Editor: Rosemary Hutchinson
Associate Art Directors: Linda Ford Vermie, Randall Yontz
Electronic Text Processor: Paula Forest
Test Kitchen Product Supervisor: Marilyn Cornelius
Food Stylists: Janet Herwig, Lisa Golden Schroeder
Photographers: Mike Dieter, M. Jensen Photography

BETTER HOMES AND GARDENS® BOOKS
An Imprint of Meredith® Books
Vice President and Editorial Director: Elizabeth P. Rice
Food and Family Life Editor: Sharyl Heiken
Art Director: Ernest Shelton
Managing Editor: David A. Kirchner
Art Production Director: John Berg
Test Kitchen Director: Sharon Stilwell

President, Book Group: Joseph J. Ward
Vice President, Retail Marketing: Jamie L. Martin
Vice President, Book Clubs: Richard L. Rundall

On the cover: Grilled Chicken and Vegetable Salad
with Chunky Salsa (see recipe, page 100)

WE CARE!

All of us at Better Homes and Gardens® Books are dedicated to
providing you with the information and ideas you need to create tasty
foods. We welcome your comments or suggestions. Write us at:
Better Homes and Gardens® Books, Cookbook Editorial Department,
LS-348, 1716 Locust Street, Des Moines IA 50309-3023.

Our seal assures you that every recipe in
Salads has been tested in the Better Homes
and Gardens® Test Kitchen. This means that
each recipe is practical and reliable, and
meets our high standards of taste appeal. We
guarantee your satisfaction with this book for
as long as you own it.

©Copyright 1992 by Meredith Corporation, Des Moines, Iowa.
All Rights Reserved. Printed in the United States of America.
First Edition. Printing Number and Year: 5 4 3 2 1   96 95 94 93 92
Library of Congress Catalog Card Number: 91-62189
ISBN: 0-696-01973-6

A salad isn't just a bowl of iceberg lettuce anymore—it's an eating adventure and anything but predictable. With the myriad of greens at our fingertips, the wider availability of fresh produce and herbs, and the renewed interest in edible flowers, salad chefs everywhere are turning over a new leaf.

More than a simple side dish, a salad can be a light appetizer or a substantial meal. It can be tossed together or artfully arranged. It can be cold, frozen, or a combination of warm meat or poultry atop chilled greens.

*And Better Homes and Gardens® **Salads** has it all—from classics such as Cobb Salad and Layered 24-Hour Salad to international salads such as Tabbouleh and Thai Chicken Salad. You'll find appetizer salads, hearty whole-meal salads, and quick-and-easy salads (made with five ingredients or less), plus dozens of pasta, potato, and fruit side salads. You'll even find some sweeter salads that can double as dessert. And what about salad dressings? **Salads** includes all the traditional favorites and some contemporary combinations, each guaranteed to enhance any salad. Recipes for an assortment of yummy breads—terrific salad companions—round out the book.*

So, survey our selection of tempting salads. You may be surprised at just how versatile and fresh-tasting a salad can be.

Contents

The Making Of a Salad

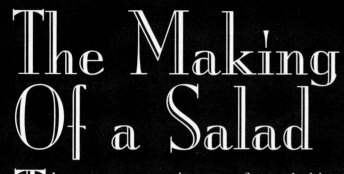

The secret to creating a perfect salad is using the freshest fruits, vegetables, and seasonings in just the right combination. To help you put together the delicious salads in this book, start with our visual glossary of salad ingredients and important tips for cleaning, storing, and preparing salad greens.

The Making of a Salad

Watercress
Small, round, delicate leaves on edible stems; peppery flavor.

Curly endive (Chicory)
Frilly, narrow, prickly leaves with a pleasantly bitter tang. Baby curly endive has a softer texture than mature curly endive.

Butterhead lettuce
Small, loosely packed leaves; subtly sweet, buttery flavor. Boston and Bibb lettuce are butterhead varieties. Bibb lettuce is slightly darker and has a smaller head than Boston. Red-tip butterhead also is available.

Escarole
Broad, irregularly shaped, flat leaves with slightly curled edges; firm, chewy texture with mildly bitter flavor.

Salad savoy (flowering kale)
Large, frilly leaves that can be purple, pink, green, or creamy white; cabbagelike flavor.

Belgian endive
Long, slender, creamy white leaves with pale yellow tips; slightly bitter flavor. Red-tip Belgian endive also is available.

8

Mesclun
Mixture of piquant and delicate baby lettuces grown in rows next to each other and harvested at the same time. The number and proportion of lettuce is seasonal and varied, but it always is a combination of flavors, textures, and colors.

Radicchio
Ruby-red leaves with thick, white veins that form a small, round, compact head; bitter and peppery tasting.

Oak-leaf lettuce
Loose, deeply cut, divided leaves that look similar to oak leaves; crisp, yet tender texture with a delicate flavor. Red oak-leaf lettuce also is available.

Arugula
Small, slender leaves similar in appearance to dandelion greens; a pungent, peppery flavor.

Spinach
Crinkled or smooth-textured leaves with long stems; somewhat earthy flavor.

Sorrel
Smooth, arrow-shaped leaves; crisp, yet tender texture with a sharp, lemonlike tang.

9

The Making of a Salad

Swiss chard
Long, flat, celerylike stalks with large, coarse leaves at the top. Red Swiss chard, also known as rhubarb chard, has ruby-colored stalks. The stems of both have a delicate, celerylike taste, and the leaves have a hearty, spinach flavor.

Kale
Frilly leaves; tough texture with a cabbagelike flavor.

Leaf lettuce
Sprawling, curly, crisp, yet tender leaves; sweet and delicate flavor. Red-tip leaf lettuce also is available.

Iceberg lettuce
Compact, smooth, round head with crisp leaves that vary from pale green in the center to medium green on the outside; mild, watery flavor.

Romaine
Large, elongated, sturdy leaves that branch from a white base; slightly sharp flavor. Red-tip romaine also is available.

Chinese cabbage (Napa)
Elongated, tightly packed, ruffly leaves with wide stalks; mild, sweet flavor.

Red cabbage
Round with very tightly packed reddish purple leaves; tastes similar to green cabbage.

Green cabbage
Round with very tightly packed pale green leaves; crisp and mild flavored.

The Making of a Salad

Chives (with flowers) (Allium schoenoprasum)
Globe-shaped lavender flowers with a mild onion flavor; grasslike, round, hollow leaves with a mild onion flavor.

Nasturtiums (Tropaeolum majus)
Yellow, red, and orange flowers with a peppery, radishlike flavor; edible leaves.

Pansies (Viola x wittrockiana)
Soft, velvety flowers in many colors with a slightly spicy flavor.

Violets and violas (Viola species)
Small, bluish purple flowers with a sweet, spicy, sometimes tangy flavor; edible leaves and stems.

Rose petals (Rosa species)
Red, pink, white, and yellow flowers with a velvety texture and a delicate, sweet flavor.

Calendulas (Calendula officinalis)
Yellow or gold flowers with a mild peppery taste.

Marigolds (Tagetes species)
Yellow and orange flowers with a mild peppery taste; *do not* eat leaves or stems.

Borage (Borago officinalis)
Purple and pink flowers with a sweet, cucumberlike flavor; edible, fuzzy, gray-green leaves that also taste like a cucumber.

Dianthus (Dianthus species)
Flat red, pink, or white flowers, some in two colors with a spicy, clovelike flavor and aroma.

Daylilies (Hemerocallis hybrids)
Flowers in many shades of orange and yellow with a slightly sweet, nutlike flavor.

Geraniums (Pelargonium species)
Pink, red, white, or purple flowers. Some varieties have flavored leaves, such as rose, lemon, mint, apple, and nutmeg.

Tarragon
Slender, dark green leaves; spicy, sharp flavor with licoricelike overtones.

Mint
Many varieties, each with different leaves. Spearmint, with light green, serrated, oval leaves, and peppermint, with darker, smoother leaves are the most popular. All varieties taste sweet, cool, and refreshing. Recipes in this book were tested with spearmint, but any variety will taste delicious.

Summer savory
Small, narrow, pointed leaves; warm, peppery flavor and grassy fragrance.

Oregano
Small, pointed leaves; strong, spicy flavor with bitter undertones.

Cilantro
Flat, serrated leaves; pungent, almost musty fragrance and taste.

Choose Edible Flowers with Care The best edible flowers are unsprayed blossoms from your own garden. Edible flowers also can be obtained from the produce section of some supermarkets, local herb gardens, some restaurant or produce suppliers, and mail-order outlets.

Not all flowers and not all parts of all flowering plants are edible. Choose only those specified on page 12 or ones you know to be safe. Use flowers that have been grown without the use of pesticides or other chemicals. Do not use flowers from florist shops—they're usually treated with chemicals.

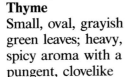

Dill
Tiny, feathery, bright green leaves; delicate, refreshing taste.

Thyme
Small, oval, grayish green leaves; heavy, spicy aroma with a pungent, clovelike taste.

Basil
Wide, oval, silky leaves with creases; flavor ranges from peppery and robust to sweet and spicy.

Italian parsley
Large, flat, dark green leaves; celerylike flavor.

Rosemary
Leathery, spiky leaves; pungent, piny flavor with a sweet scent.

The Making of a Salad

Summer squash
Baby zucchini: Slender, elongated squash with green skin and off-white meat; mildly sweet flavor. A globe-shaped variety also is available.
Baby pattypan: Scalloped squash with a flat, round shape, pale green or white skin, and off-white meat; mildly sweet flavor.
Baby sunburst: Scalloped squash with bright yellow skin and off-white meat; mildly sweet flavor.

Artichoke
Globe-shaped bud with sharp, pointed leaves that grows on a tall, thistlelike plant; subtle, nutty flavor.

White asparagus
Creamy white tender spears with a mild flavor and delicate texture. They are harvested when the tips just break ground; the lack of exposure to light keeps the spears white. White asparagus, more expensive than green, also is available in canned form.

Tomato
Yellow: Yellow-skinned tomato with yellow meat, a firm, juicy texture, and the familiar tomato flavor.
Plum-shaped: Medium to small, oval-shaped, red or yellow tomato; meaty texture with small seeds, little juice, and a mild, rich flavor.
Baby pear-shaped: Bite-size red or yellow tomato that resembles a miniature pear; mild, sweet flavor.
Sun-dried: Dried tomatoes with a salty flavor; often packed in oil.

Bok choy
Long, white, celerylike stalks and large, deep green leaves; crisp like celery with a sweet, mild, cabbagelike flavor. It is a variety of Chinese cabbage.

Mango
Oval, round, or kidney-shaped tropical fruit with green to yellow skin tinged with red; deep golden yellow meat with a large, flat, oval, white seed; spicy, peachlike flavor; very juicy.

Mushrooms
Shiitake: Brown, slender stem with a large, floppy cap; rich, meaty flavor. Because the stem is tough, use only the cap.
Morel: Resembles an irregularly shaped sponge; golden brown; hearty flavor; tender texture.
Enoki: Long, slender stem and tiny cap; stem is attached to a central base; mild flavor.
Straw: Brown and umbrella-shaped; mild flavor; meaty texture. It is grown on straw made from rice plants.

Baby corn
Tiny version of corn on the cob with the same mild, sweet flavor. The cob is edible.

Fiddlehead fern
Young, edible, tightly curled, green shoot of a fern; tastes like a cross between green beans and asparagus with the texture of green beans.

Celeriac
Irregular, brown-skinned, knobby root vegetable with a creamy white interior; mild, celerylike flavor with a crisp, turniplike texture. It also is called celery root.

Papaya
Melonlike, pear-shaped fruit with greenish yellow to yellow-orange skin and golden orange meat; tastes like a cross between peaches and melons. It is fragrant and sweet with a creamy, spoonable consistency.

Leek
Resembles an oversized green onion with overlapping, wide, green leaves; a fat, white stalk with shaggy roots at bulb end. It is a member of the onion family and has a subtle onion flavor.

Tangelo
Cross between a tangerine and grapefruit; oval to round in shape; light to deep orange skin that peels easily; pale yellow to deep orange meat; tangy, sweet, orange flavor; juicy with few seeds.

Heart of palm
Cream-colored interior of a young palm tree; resembles thick stalks of white asparagus; silky texture; delicate flavor reminiscent of artichokes. It rarely is available fresh.

Jicama
Large, tuberous root vegetable; pale brown, thin skin; crisp, white, potatolike meat; mildly sweet flavor.

Lemongrass
Lemon-flavored plant resembling a fibrous green onion. It can be purchased fresh or dried.

15

to remove any dirt or sand particles. After a few minutes, lift the greens out and discard the water. Dunk the greens repeatedly until no more dirt or sand collects in the bowl.

For greens with stems, break off and discard the stems. (Greens such as spinach, Swiss chard, sorrel, arugula, watercress, and mustard greens have stems.) For romaine, cut out heavy center vein.

Cleaning the greens

Handling greens properly from the time you buy them until the time you're ready to toss them in a salad assures that your salads will be crisp and flavorful.

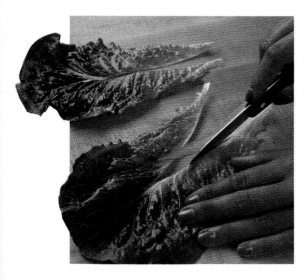

When you bring lettuce and other greens home, wash them thoroughly before storing them. Remove and discard any outer leaves that are bruised, discolored, tough, or wilted.

To clean iceberg lettuce, loosen the core by hitting the stem end sharply on the countertop. Then twist the core and lift it out. Don't use a knife because the cut edges of the lettuce will turn a rusty color. Wash iceberg lettuce by holding the head, core side up, under cold running water. Rinse the lettuce thoroughly, then invert the head and let it drain.

To clean leaf lettuce, romaine, Boston lettuce, Bibb lettuce, and curly endive, cut off the bottom core. Then wash the leaves under cold running water.

Place spinach, watercress, arugula, and other greens with small leaves in a large bowl of cold water

Drying the greens

Any water that clings to the greens dilutes the flavor and consistency of the salad dressing you use and

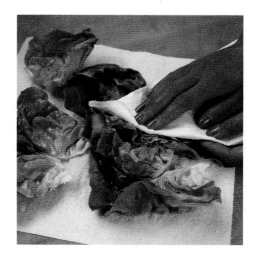

makes the salad soggy. Excess moisture also will cause stored greens to deteriorate quickly. To avoid watery salads, drain the greens in a colander. Then place the greens on a clean kitchen towel or several layers of paper towels. Place a second towel or more paper towels over the greens. Gently pat the greens dry. Or, use a salad spinner. Place the greens in the basket and turn the handle to spin the greens dry.

Crisping and storing greens

Wrap dried greens in a dry kitchen towel or paper towels and refrigerate them for at least 30 minutes or up to several hours to crisp.

If you're not planning to use the greens right away, place the wrapped greens in a plastic bag or an airtight container. When properly stored, greens generally stay crisp for 3 or 4 days (arugula and watercress will probably only stay fresh for up to 2 days, however).

Tearing greens

For bite-size pieces, tear lettuce leaves. Tearing rather than cutting avoids bruising and browning the leaves. It also exposes more of the insides of the leaves, so the leaves absorb salad dressing better.

Adding the dressing

To avoid damp, soggy salads, add dressing just before serving. Add only enough dressing to lightly coat the leaves. Too much dressing

masks the flavors of the greens; too little dressing and the salad is tasteless. Toss the salad and dressing with two salad servers or spoons. Gently push downward to the bottom of a deep bowl with both salad servers and lift up and over. Don't be too enthusiastic when tossing the salad or you'll bruise the tender leaves.

For arranged salads, drizzle the dressing over the arrangement or serve the dressing separately.

All-American Salads

Here's a collection
of taste-tempting traditional
American salads ranging from celebrated restaurant
classics such as Cobb Salad to home-style
favorites such as Mixed Bean Salad. No matter what
the occasion, one of these tasty salads will fill
the bill.

TACO SALAD

As an option to the greens, cut flour tortillas into wedges or fun shapes. Place them on a baking sheet and bake them in a 350° oven about 10 minutes.

1 pound ground beef **or** *ground raw turkey*

3 cloves garlic, minced

1 16-ounce can dark red kidney beans

1 8-ounce jar taco sauce

1 tablespoon chili powder

2 cups chopped tomatoes (4 medium)

2 cups shredded cheddar cheese (8 ounces)

1 cup chopped green pepper (1 large)

½ cup sliced pitted ripe olives

¼ cup sliced green onion (4 medium)

Leaf lettuce leaves

White salad savoy leaves

1 medium avocado, seeded, peeled, and sliced (optional)

Lime wedges (optional)

Dairy sour cream (optional)

Salsa **or** *taco sauce (optional)*

For meat mixture, in a large skillet cook beef or turkey and garlic till meat is no longer pink. Drain off fat. Stir in *undrained* kidney beans, taco sauce, and chili powder. Bring to boiling; reduce heat. Cover and simmer for 10 minutes.

❧

Meanwhile, in a large mixing bowl combine tomatoes, cheese, green pepper, olives, and green onion; add hot meat mixture. Toss lightly to mix. Line 6 salad plates with lettuce and salad savoy leaves. Divide salad mixture among plates. Garnish with avocado and lime wedges, if desired. Serve with sour cream and salsa or additional taco sauce, if desired. Makes 6 main-dish servings.

Time

Start to finish   25 min.

Per Serving

Calories	*407*
Protein	*30 g*
Carbohydrate	*22 g*
Total Fat	*23 g*
Saturated Fat	*12 g*
Cholesterol	*87 mg*
Sodium	*800 mg*
Potassium	*737 mg*

Our taste panel loved this extra-creamy potato salad. One editor described its taste as "just like my Mom's."

Classic Potato Salad

6 medium potatoes (2 pounds)

1¼ cups mayonnaise **or** salad dressing

1 tablespoon prepared mustard (optional)

½ teaspoon salt

¼ teaspoon pepper

1 cup thinly sliced celery (2 stalks)

½ cup chopped onion (1 medium)

½ cup chopped sweet pickle **or** sweet pickle relish

6 hard-cooked eggs, coarsely chopped

Lettuce leaves

Paprika (optional)

Time

Preparation	45 min.
Chilling	6 to 24 hrs.

Per Serving

Calories	280
Protein	5 g
Carbohydrate	19 g
Total Fat	21 g
Saturated Fat	4 g
Cholesterol	120 mg
Sodium	333 mg
Potassium	357 mg

In a covered saucepan cook potatoes in boiling water for 12 to 15 minutes or till just tender; drain well. Cool slightly. Peel and cube potatoes.

Meanwhile, for dressing, in a small mixing bowl stir together mayonnaise or salad dressing, mustard (if desired), salt, and pepper.

In a large mixing bowl combine dressing, celery, onion, and sweet pickle or pickle relish. Add potatoes and hard-cooked eggs. Toss lightly to coat. Cover and chill for 6 to 24 hours.

To serve, line a salad bowl with lettuce leaves. Transfer potato salad to the lettuce-lined bowl. Sprinkle with paprika, if desired. Makes 12 side-dish servings.

Mixed Bean Salad

1 15-ounce can garbanzo beans, drained, **or** one 16-ounce can cut wax beans, drained

1 8-ounce can red kidney beans, drained

1 8-ounce can cut green beans, drained

½ cup chopped onion (1 medium)

½ cup chopped green pepper (1 small)

½ cup shredded carrot (1 medium)

¼ cup sliced pitted ripe olives

½ cup vinegar

¼ cup salad oil

2 tablespoons sugar

1½ teaspoons snipped fresh basil **or** ½ teaspoon dried basil, crushed

1½ teaspoons snipped fresh oregano **or** ½ teaspoon dried oregano, crushed

½ teaspoon dry mustard

⅛ teaspoon pepper

1 clove garlic, minced

Lettuce leaves

In a large mixing bowl combine garbanzo beans or wax beans, kidney beans, green beans, onion, green pepper, carrot, and olives.

❧

For marinade, in a screw-top jar combine vinegar, oil, sugar, basil, oregano, dry mustard, pepper, and garlic. Cover and shake well. Pour marinade over bean mixture. Cover and chill for 4 to 24 hours, stirring occasionally.

❧

To serve, line a salad bowl with lettuce leaves. Using a slotted spoon, transfer the bean salad from the marinade to the lettuce-lined bowl. Makes 6 side-dish servings.

Watching your sodium intake? If so, rinse the canned beans before adding them to the other vegetables.

Time

Preparation	20 min.
Marinating	4 to 24 hrs.

Per Serving

Calories	238
Protein	8 g
Carbohydrate	30 g
Total Fat	11 g
Saturated Fat	1 g
Cholesterol	0 mg
Sodium	199 mg
Potassium	404 mg

For a change of pace, we switched from the traditional apples to pears in our rendition of Waldorf Salad. *The sweet, crisp pears and the whipped cream dressing make a perfect match.*

WALDORF SALAD

2 cups chopped pears or *chopped apples (2 medium)*

1½ teaspoons lemon juice

⅓ cup slivered almonds or *chopped pecans, toasted*

¼ cup celery

¼ cup dried cherries or *raisins*

¼ cup seedless grapes, halved

⅓ cup whipping cream

¼ cup mayonnaise or *salad dressing*

In a medium mixing bowl toss chopped pears or apples with lemon juice. Stir in nuts, celery, cherries or raisins, and grapes.

❧

For dressing, in a chilled small mixing bowl whip cream to soft peaks. Fold mayonnaise or salad dressing into the whipped cream. Fold dressing into fruit mixture. Cover and chill for 2 to 24 hours. Makes 4 to 6 side-dish servings.

Time

Preparation	20 min.
Chilling	2 to 24 hrs.

Per Serving

Calories	317
Protein	4 g
Carbohydrate	24 g
Total Fat	24 g
Saturated Fat	7 g
Cholesterol	35 mg
Sodium	94 mg
Potassium	247 mg

Toasting Nuts and Sesame Seed

As you look through this book, you'll notice that many of the recipes call for toasted pecans, walnuts, almonds, and sesame seed. Toasted nuts and sesame seed taste richer than untoasted ones, and retain a crisp texture when added to salads.

To toast nuts or sesame seed, spread them in a thin layer in a shallow baking pan. Bake them in a 350° oven for 5 to 10 minutes, or till they are a light golden brown, stirring once or twice. Let them cool before adding them to your salad.

TODAY'S CAESAR SALAD

1 egg

⅓ cup chicken broth

3 anchovy fillets

3 tablespoons olive oil

2 tablespoons lemon juice

Few dashes white wine Worcestershire sauce

1 clove garlic, halved

10 cups torn romaine

½ cup Parmesan Croutons (see recipe, page 231) **or** purchased garlic croutons

¼ cup grated Parmesan cheese

Whole black peppercorns

For dressing, in a blender container or food processor bowl combine egg, chicken broth, anchovy fillets, olive oil, lemon juice, and Worcestershire sauce. Cover and blend or process till smooth. Transfer dressing to a small saucepan. Cook and stir dressing over low heat for 8 to 10 minutes or till thickened. *Do not boil.* Transfer to a bowl. Cover surface with plastic wrap; chill for 2 to 24 hours.

※

To serve, rub the inside of a wooden salad bowl with the cut sides of the garlic clove; discard garlic clove. Add romaine, croutons, and Parmesan cheese to salad bowl. Pour dressing over salad. Toss lightly to coat. Transfer to individual salad plates. Grind peppercorns over each serving. Makes 6 side-dish servings.

Our updated version of Caesar salad features a cooked egg dressing instead of the traditional uncooked dressing. Using uncooked eggs in recipes such as this may lead to bacterial contamination.

Time

Preparation	*15 min.*
Chilling	*2 to 24 hrs.*

Per Serving

Calories	*149*
Protein	*6 g*
Carbohydrate	*6 g*
Total Fat	*12 g*
Saturated Fat	*3 g*
Cholesterol	*46 mg*
Sodium	*259 mg*
Potassium	*323 mg*

Time

Preparation	20 min.
Chilling	2 to 24 hrs.

Per Serving

Calories	233
Protein	2 g
Carbohydrate	9 g
Total Fat	22 g
Saturated Fat	3 g
Cholesterol	17 mg
Sodium	179 mg
Potassium	273 mg

Vinaigrette Coleslaw:

Calories	132
Protein	1 g
Carbohydrate	11 g
Total Fat	10 g
Saturated Fat	1 g
Cholesterol	0 mg
Sodium	21 mg
Potassium	266 mg

CREAMY COLESLAW

½ cup mayonnaise or *salad dressing*

1 tablespoon milk

1 to 2 teaspoons sugar

½ teaspoon celery seed

3 cups shredded green cabbage

1 cup shredded red cabbage

1 cup shredded carrot (2 medium)

For dressing, in a small mixing bowl stir together mayonnaise or salad dressing, milk, sugar, and celery seed.

❧

In a large mixing bowl combine green cabbage, red cabbage, and shredded carrot. Pour the dressing over the cabbage mixture. Toss lightly to coat. Cover and chill for 2 to 24 hours. Makes 4 side-dish servings.

VINAIGRETTE COLESLAW

Prepare as above, *except* substitute vinaigrette for dressing. For vinaigrette, in a screw-top jar combine 3 tablespoons *vinegar,* 3 tablespoons *salad oil,* 1 to 2 tablespoons *sugar,* and, if desired, ¼ teaspoon *caraway seed.* Cover and shake well.

WILTED ROMAINE SALAD

6 cups torn romaine or *spinach*

1 cup sliced fresh mushrooms

¼ cup sliced green onion (4 medium)

3 slices bacon

3 tablespoons vinegar

1 teaspoon sugar

¼ teaspoon dry mustard

1 cup sliced nectarines or *sliced, peeled peaches (2 medium)*

1 hard-cooked egg, chopped

In a large mixing bowl combine romaine or spinach, mushrooms, and green onion. Set aside.

❧

In a 12-inch skillet cook bacon over medium heat till crisp. Remove bacon, reserving drippings in skillet. Drain bacon on paper towels. Crumble bacon and set aside. Stir vinegar, sugar, and mustard into reserved drippings; bring just to boiling.

❧

Add the romaine mixture to skillet. Toss for 30 to 60 seconds or till romaine is just wilted. Remove from heat. Add nectarine or peach slices. Toss lightly to mix. Transfer to a serving bowl. Sprinkle with egg and crumbled bacon. Serve immediately. Makes 4 side-dish servings.

Nectarine slices, romaine, and a hot bacon and vinegar dressing team up for a zesty sweet-and-sour salad.

Time

Start to finish 25 min.

Per Serving

Calories	*90*
Protein	*5 g*
Carbohydrate	*9 g*
Total Fat	*4 g*
Saturated Fat	*1 g*
Cholesterol	*57 mg*
Sodium	*100 mg*
Potassium	*450 mg*

25

Developed at the Brown Derby Restaurant in Los Angeles, this chicken and avocado salad now appears on menus throughout the country.

COBB SALAD

6 cups shredded red Swiss chard **or** *shredded lettuce*

3 cups chopped cooked chicken

1½ cups chopped, seeded tomatoes (2 medium)

¾ cup crumbled blue cheese (3 ounces)

6 slices bacon, crisp-cooked, drained, and crumbled

3 hard-cooked eggs, chopped

1 small head Belgian endive

1 medium avocado, seeded, peeled, and cut into wedges

Pineapple sage flower (optional)

Brown Derby French Dressing

Arrange shredded Swiss chard or lettuce on 6 salad plates. Evenly divide chicken, tomatoes, cheese, bacon, and eggs among the plates; arrange ingredients in a star shape atop the lettuce. Separate the Belgian endive into leaves. Place a few endive leaves on one side of each plate. Top each salad with avocado wedges. Garnish with a pineapple sage flower, if desired. Serve with Brown Derby French Dressing. Makes 6 main-dish servings.

BROWN DERBY FRENCH DRESSING

In a screw-top jar combine ½ cup *olive oil or salad oil,* ⅓ cup *red wine vinegar,* 1 tablespoon *lemon juice,* 1 teaspoon *Worcestershire sauce,* ½ teaspoon *salt,* ½ teaspoon *sugar,* ½ teaspoon *dry mustard,* ½ teaspoon *pepper,* and 1 clove *garlic,* minced. Cover and shake well. Shake before serving. Makes about 1 cup.

Time

Start to finish   25 min.

Per Serving

Calories	496
Protein	32 g
Carbohydrate	11 g
Total Fat	36 g
Saturated Fat	9 g
Cholesterol	181 mg
Sodium	597 mg
Potassium	726 mg

Originally a side dish popular with German immigrants in America, today this tangy salad is an all-American favorite.

Time

Start to finish   45 min.

Per Serving

Calories	295
Protein	9 g
Carbohydrate	37 g
Total Fat	13 g
Saturated Fat	4 g
Cholesterol	125 mg
Sodium	493 mg
Potassium	701 mg

GERMAN HOT POTATO SALAD

10 to 12 small red potatoes (about 1 pound)

*1 medium green **or** sweet red pepper, cut into bite-size pieces (1 cup)*

½ cup chopped celery (1 stalk)

2 tablespoons snipped parsley

4 slices bacon

½ cup chopped onion (1 medium)

1 tablespoon all-purpose flour

1 tablespoon sugar

½ teaspoon salt

½ teaspoon celery seed

½ teaspoon dry mustard

¼ teaspoon pepper

½ cup water

¼ cup vinegar

2 hard-cooked eggs, sliced

In a covered saucepan cook potatoes in boiling water for 12 to 15 minutes or till just tender; drain well. Cool slightly. Cut potatoes into ¼-inch-thick slices. In a large mixing bowl combine potatoes, pepper strips, celery, and parsley. Set aside.

For dressing, in a large skillet cook bacon over medium heat till crisp. Remove bacon, reserving *2 tablespoons* drippings in skillet. Drain bacon on paper towels. Crumble bacon and set aside. Add chopped onion to reserved drippings. Cook over medium heat till onion is tender but not brown. Stir in flour, sugar, salt, celery seed, dry mustard, and pepper. Stir in water and vinegar. Cook and stir till thickened and bubbly.

Add potato mixture and crumbled bacon to dressing. Toss lightly to mix. Cook, stirring gently, for 2 to 3 minutes or till heated through. Transfer to a serving bowl. Garnish with hard-cooked egg slices. Makes 4 to 6 side-dish servings.

LAYERED 24-HOUR SALAD

Salad ingredients in layers stay crisp and fresh till serving time in this potluck favorite.

4 cups torn mixed greens

1 cup sliced fresh mushrooms **or** *frozen peas, thawed*

2 small tomatoes, cut into thin wedges

1 cup shredded carrot (2 medium)

½ cup thinly sliced celery (1 stalk)

½ cup sliced radishes

2 hard-cooked eggs, sliced

6 slices bacon, crisp-cooked, drained, and crumbled

¼ cup sliced green onion (4 medium)

Buttermilk-Herb Dressing (see recipe, page 207)

¾ cup shredded cheddar, American, **or** *Muenster cheese (optional)*

Place greens in the bottom of a 3-quart salad bowl. Layer in the following order: mushrooms or peas, tomato wedges, carrot, celery, radishes, egg slices, bacon, and green onion.

❧

Spread Buttermilk-Herb Dressing evenly over the top of the salad, sealing to the edge of the bowl. Sprinkle with cheese, if desired. Cover tightly with plastic wrap. Chill for 4 to 24 hours. To serve, toss lightly to mix. Makes 6 to 8 side-dish servings.

Time

Preparation	40 min.
Chilling	4 to 24 hrs.

Per Serving

Calories	365
Protein	7 g
Carbohydrate	8 g
Total Fat	35 g
Saturated Fat	6 g
Cholesterol	99 mg
Sodium	392 mg
Potassium	421 mg

Choose any small pasta such as corkscrew macaroni, small shells, or tiny bow ties.

MACARONI SALAD

1 cup elbow macaroni or wagon wheel macaroni (3 ounces)

¾ cup cubed cheddar or American cheese (3 ounces)

½ cup thinly sliced celery (1 stalk)

½ cup frozen peas

½ cup sliced radishes

2 tablespoons sliced green onion or chopped onion

½ cup mayonnaise or salad dressing

¼ cup sweet pickle relish or chopped sweet pickle

2 tablespoons milk

¼ teaspoon salt

Dash ground pepper

2 hard-cooked eggs, coarsely chopped

Time

Preparation	30 min.
Chilling	4 to 24 hrs.

Per Serving

Calories	313
Protein	9 g
Carbohydrate	21 g
Total Fat	22 g
Saturated Fat	6 g
Cholesterol	97 mg
Sodium	401 mg
Potassium	180 mg

Cook pasta according to package directions. Drain pasta. Rinse with *cold* water; drain again.

❧

In a large mixing bowl combine pasta, cheese, celery, peas, radishes, and onion.

❧

For dressing, in a small mixing bowl stir together mayonnaise or salad dressing, pickle relish or chopped sweet pickle, milk, salt, and pepper. Pour dressing over pasta mixture. Add hard-cooked eggs. Toss lightly to coat. Cover and chill for 4 to 24 hours. Before serving, if necessary, stir in additional milk to moisten. Makes 6 side-dish servings.

CHEF'S SALAD

You make the choice. Select the meat, poultry, cheese, and dressing you like best.

---

3 cups torn iceberg lettuce **or** *leaf lettuce*

3 cups torn romaine **or** *spinach*

4 ounces fully cooked ham, chicken, turkey, beef, pork, **or** *lamb, cut into thin strips*

1 cup cubed Swiss, cheddar, American, provolone, **or** *Gruyère cheese*

or *crumbled blue cheese (4 ounces)*

2 hard-cooked eggs, sliced

2 medium tomatoes, cut into wedges, **or** *8 cherry tomatoes, halved*

1 small green **or** *sweet red pepper, cut into rings*

3 tablespoons sliced green onion (3 medium)

1 cup Parmesan Croutons (see recipe, page 231) **or** *purchased croutons (optional)*

¾ cup Creamy Herb Dressing (see recipe, page 208), Buttermilk-Herb Dressing (see recipe, page 207), Creamy Italian Dressing (see recipe, page 206), **or** *other salad dressing*

In a large salad bowl toss together lettuce and romaine or spinach. Arrange meat or poultry, cheese, hard-cooked eggs, tomatoes, pepper rings, and green onion over the greens. Sprinkle with Parmesan Croutons, if desired. Pour Creamy Herb Dressing or other salad dressing over salad. Toss lightly to coat. Makes 4 main-dish servings.

INDIVIDUAL CHEF'S SALADS

Prepare Chef's Salad as above, *except* divide lettuce mixture among 4 salad bowls. Top *each* serving with *one-fourth* of the meat or poultry, cheese, hard-cooked eggs, tomatoes, pepper rings, and green onion. Sprinkle *each* with *one-fourth* of the Parmesan Croutons, if desired. Serve with Creamy Herb Dressing or other salad dressing.

Time

Start to finish   40 min.

Per Serving

Calories	*357*
Protein	*21 g*
Carbohydrate	*10 g*
Total Fat	*27 g*
Saturated Fat	*10 g*
Cholesterol	*162 mg*
Sodium	*661 mg*
Potassium	*574 mg*

International Salads

Cooks around the world combine locally grown fruits and vegetables to make fascinating salads. This chapter provides a sampling of some of the best-known international salads. Recipes for favorites such as Thai Chicken Salad and Indonesian Gado-Gado can be found on the following pages. So for a special meal, choose a country and showcase its cuisine with one of these luscious salads.

ENSALADA DE NOCHEBUENA

Borrow a tradition from Mexico and serve this refreshing fruit salad on Christmas Eve.

2 medium oranges

2 cups fresh cubed pineapple **or** *one 20-ounce can pineapple chunks (juice pack), drained*

1 large apple, cored and sliced

1 medium banana, sliced

⅓ cup olive oil

3 tablespoons vinegar

2 tablespoons lime juice

2 tablespoons sugar

Romaine leaves

4 cups shredded leaf lettuce

1 16-ounce can sliced beets, rinsed and drained

1 cup jicama cut into julienne strips

½ cup pine nuts **or** *peanuts*

½ cup finely chopped red onion **or** *pomegranate seeds*

Fresh cilantro (optional)

Time

Preparation	15 min.
Chilling	2 to 24 hrs.
Assembling	15 min.

Peel and section oranges over a bowl to catch the juice. Add orange sections, pineapple, apple, and banana to the bowl. Toss to coat all the fruit with orange juice. Cover; chill 2 to 24 hours.

❧

For dressing, in a screw-top jar combine olive oil, vinegar, lime juice, and sugar. Cover and shake well.

❧

To serve, line 6 salad plates with romaine leaves. Top with shredded lettuce. Drain the fruit mixture. Divide the fruit mixture, beets, and jicama among the salad plates. Sprinkle each serving with pine nuts or peanuts and chopped onion or pomegranate seeds. Shake dressing well; pour over each salad. Garnish with cilantro, if desired. Makes 6 side-dish servings.

Per Serving

Calories	289
Protein	5 g
Carbohydrate	35 g
Total Fat	18 g
Saturated Fat	2 g
Cholesterol	0 mg
Sodium	143 mg
Potassium	571 mg

This simple salad features foods typical of Spanish cuisine— tomatoes, peppers, olives, and olive oil.

Time

Preparation	15 min.
Chilling	1 to 4 hrs.

Per Serving

Calories	156
Protein	1 g
Carbohydrate	7 g
Total Fat	15 g
Saturated Fat	2 g
Cholesterol	0 mg
Sodium	187 mg
Potassium	227 mg

SPANISH TOMATO SALAD

2 medium tomatoes, sliced

1 medium green **or** *sweet red pepper, cut into strips*

½ of a medium onion, thinly sliced and separated into rings

¼ cup sliced pitted green **or** *ripe olives*

¼ cup olive oil

¼ cup vinegar

1 clove garlic, minced

½ teaspoon pepper

2 tablespoons snipped cilantro **or** *parsley*

In a large mixing bowl combine tomato slices, pepper strips, onion rings, and olives.

For marinade, in a screw-top jar combine olive oil, vinegar, garlic, and pepper. Cover and shake well. Pour marinade over the tomato mixture. Cover and chill for 1 to 4 hours, stirring occasionally.

To serve, use a slotted spoon to divide the marinated vegetables among 4 salad plates. Sprinkle each serving with cilantro or parsley. Makes 4 side-dish servings.

SICILIAN SALAD

1 medium eggplant (about 1 pound)

3 tablespoons olive oil

2 medium sweet red, green, **or** yellow peppers

3 tablespoons red wine vinegar

1 clove garlic, minced

1 teaspoon snipped fresh basil **or** ¼ teaspoon dried basil, crushed

½ teaspoon salt

¼ teaspoon pepper

2 medium tomatoes, halved lengthwise and sliced

Cut the eggplant in half lengthwise. Reserve one half for another use. Cut the remaining eggplant half into ½-inch-thick slices. Place the eggplant slices on a foil-lined baking sheet. Brush with *1 tablespoon* of the olive oil.

❧

Quarter the peppers lengthwise. Remove stems and seeds. Cut small slits into the ends of the pepper pieces to make them lie flat. Place the pepper pieces, cut sides down, on the foil-lined baking sheet.

❧

Bake in a 425° oven for 15 minutes or till eggplant is tender. Remove eggplant from baking sheet. Bake pepper pieces for 5 to 10 minutes more or till skins are bubbly and brown. Immediately place pepper pieces in a clean brown paper bag. Close bag tightly; cool. Peel the cooled pepper pieces with a sharp knife. Cut lengthwise into ½-inch-wide strips. In a large mixing bowl combine eggplant and pepper strips.

❧

For marinade, in a screw-top jar combine the remaining 2 tablespoons olive oil, the vinegar, garlic, basil, salt, and pepper. Cover and shake well. Pour dressing over pepper mixture. Toss lightly to coat. Cover and chill for 4 to 24 hours, stirring occasionally.

❧

To serve, stir tomatoes into the pepper mixture. Serve with a slotted spoon. Makes 4 side-dish servings.

Marinated salads, such as this eggplant and pepper salad, often are part of an antipasto tray in Sicily.

Time

Preparation	50 min.
Chilling	4 to 24 hrs.

Per Serving

Calories	128
Protein	1 g
Carbohydrate	9 g
Total Fat	11 g
Saturated Fat	1 g
Cholesterol	0 mg
Sodium	278 mg
Potassium	323 mg

In Greece, this simple tossed salad appears frequently on menus where it's called Village Salad, Summer Salad, or Peasant Salad.

GREEK SALAD

2 cups torn romaine

1 cup torn escarole or curly endive

1 medium tomato

½ of a medium red onion

1 small green, sweet yellow, or sweet red pepper, cut into strips

¼ cup sliced radishes

¼ cup sliced Greek olives or pitted ripe olives

Greek Vinaigrette

½ cup crumbled feta cheese (2 ounces)

In a large salad bowl combine romaine and escarole or endive; set aside.

Cut the tomato into thin wedges; cut each wedge in half. Slice the onion; cut each slice in half. Add tomato, onion, pepper strips, sliced radishes, and Greek or ripe olives to the greens. Shake Greek Vinaigrette well; pour over salad. Toss lightly to coat. Sprinkle with feta cheese. Makes 4 side-dish servings.

GREEK VINAIGRETTE

In a screw-top jar combine 3 tablespoons *olive oil or salad oil;* 3 tablespoons *lemon juice;* 1 tablespoon *anchovy paste;* 1 tablespoon snipped fresh *oregano or* 1 teaspoon dried *oregano,* crushed; 2 large cloves *garlic,* minced; and ⅛ teaspoon *pepper.* Cover and shake well. Makes about ½ cup.

Time

Start to finish   25 min.

Per Serving

Calories	180
Protein	6 g
Carbohydrate	8 g
Total Fat	15 g
Saturated Fat	4 g
Cholesterol	18 mg
Sodium	454 mg
Potassium	330 mg

TABBOULEH

Both Lebanon and Syria claim this fiber-rich grain salad.

¾ cup bulgur

½ cup chopped, seeded cucumber

½ cup snipped parsley

2 tablespoons sliced green onion (2 medium)

¼ cup olive oil **or** salad oil

¼ cup lemon juice

1 tablespoon snipped fresh mint **or** ½ teaspoon dried mint, crushed

¼ teaspoon salt

⅛ teaspoon pepper

½ cup chopped, seeded tomato (1 small)

Rinse bulgur in a colander with *cold* water; drain. In a medium mixing bowl combine bulgur, chopped cucumber, snipped parsley, and sliced green onion.

❧

For dressing, in a screw-top jar combine olive oil or salad oil, lemon juice, mint, salt, and pepper. Cover and shake well. Pour dressing over bulgur mixture. Toss lightly to coat. Cover and chill for 4 to 24 hours.

❧

Before serving, stir chopped tomato into bulgur mixture. Makes 4 to 6 side-dish servings.

Time

Preparation	20 min.
Chilling	4 to 24 hrs.

Per Serving

Calories	246
Protein	5 g
Carbohydrate	29 g
Total Fat	14 g
Saturated Fat	2 g
Cholesterol	0 mg
Sodium	148 mg
Potassium	561 mg

THAI CHICKEN SALAD

Look *for bean threads, sometimes called cellophane noodles, and fish sauce in an Oriental market or the Oriental section of some larger supermarkets.*

¼ cup snipped fresh cilantro

3 tablespoons soy sauce

2 tablespoons water

2 tablespoons fish sauce

2 large cloves garlic, minced

½ teaspoon pepper

2 whole large chicken breasts (about 2 pounds total), skinned, boned, and cut into 1-inch pieces

4 ounces bean threads

3 tablespoons lime juice

1½ teaspoons sugar

Lettuce leaves (optional)

2 medium tomatoes, cut into wedges

1½ cups chopped, seeded cucumber (1 medium)

3 tablespoons sliced green onion (3 medium)

1 tablespoon chopped dry roasted peanuts

4 thin lime slices

Time

Preparation	15 min.
Marinating	2 to 24 hrs.
Assembling	30 min.

Per Serving

Calories	308
Protein	36 g
Carbohydrate	30 g
Total Fat	6 g
Saturated Fat	1 g
Cholesterol	72 mg
Sodium	1,469 mg
Potassium	853 mg

In a shallow bowl combine cilantro, *2 tablespoons* of the soy sauce, water, fish sauce, garlic, and pepper. Add chicken pieces; mix well. Cover and marinate in the refrigerator for 2 to 24 hours, stirring occasionally.

In a medium mixing bowl soak bean threads for 30 minutes in enough hot water to cover. Drain well; squeeze out excess moisture. Cut into 2-inch lengths.

Drain the chicken pieces. Place chicken pieces in a heavy shallow baking pan. Broil 4 to 5 inches from the heat for 4 to 7 minutes or till tender and no longer pink, stirring once.

Meanwhile, for dressing, in a screw-top jar combine lime juice, the remaining 1 tablespoon soy sauce, and sugar. Cover and shake well.

To serve, line 4 salad plates with lettuce leaves, if desired. Arrange the bean threads atop lettuce. Divide chicken pieces, tomatoes, and cucumber among the plates. Shake dressing well; pour over chicken and vegetables. Sprinkle each serving with green onion and peanuts. Garnish with lime slices. Makes 4 main-dish servings.

GADO-GADO

½ pound firm tofu

⅓ cup salad oil

½ pound green beans

½ pound whole tiny new potatoes, quartered

2 tablespoons chopped onion

1 clove garlic, minced

2 teaspoons salad oil

½ cup coconut milk

¼ cup peanut butter

1 tablespoon diced green chili peppers

1½ teaspoons brown sugar

1 teaspoon grated gingerroot

½ teaspoon finely shredded lime peel **or** lemon peel

½ teaspoon shrimp paste

6 cups spinach leaves

1¾ cups sliced cucumber (1 medium)

1 cup bean sprouts

1 cup shredded cabbage

2 hard-cooked eggs, chopped

Arrange this Indonesian salad on a large platter for an impressive side dish, or serve it as an appetizer.

Time

Start to finish   50 min.

Per Serving

Calories	279
Protein	10 g
Carbohydrate	18 g
Total Fat	21 g
Saturated Fat	6 g
Cholesterol	54 mg
Sodium	110 mg
Potassium	706 mg

Drain tofu; cut into 1-inch cubes. In a large skillet cook the tofu in the ⅓ cup hot oil till golden. Remove tofu from skillet; drain on paper towels.

❧

Wash green beans, remove ends and strings. In a large covered saucepan cook green beans in boiling water for 20 to 25 minutes or till just tender; add potatoes for the last 12 to 15 minutes and cook till just tender. Drain; set aside.

❧

For dressing, in a small saucepan cook onion and garlic in the 2 teaspoons oil. Stir in coconut milk, peanut butter, chili peppers, brown sugar, gingerroot, lime peel or lemon peel, and shrimp paste. Cook over low heat, stirring till smooth. Remove from heat; set aside.

❧

Arrange spinach leaves on a large round or oval platter. Place the cucumber slices in a ring around the outside edge of the platter. Arrange the tofu, green beans, potatoes, bean sprouts, and cabbage in spoke-fashion inside the cucumber ring. Sprinkle the chopped egg over the salad. Stir dressing well; pour over salad. Makes 8 side-dish servings.

SALADE NIÇOISE

Pronounced sah-LAHD nee-SWAHZ, this salad comes from the South of France. Usually made with tuna, we added rosy salmon as an option for a more colorful entrée.

½ pound green beans

¾ pound whole tiny new potatoes, sliced

¼ cup olive oil **or** *salad oil*

¼ cup white wine vinegar **or** *white vinegar*

1 teaspoon sugar

1 teaspoon snipped fresh tarragon **or** *¼ teaspoon dried tarragon, crushed*

⅛ teaspoon dry mustard

Dash pepper

Boston **or** *Bibb lettuce leaves*

1½ cups flaked, cooked tuna **or** *salmon (½ pound)* **or** *one 9¼-ounce can chunk white tuna (water pack), drained and broken into chunks*

2 medium tomatoes, cut into wedges

2 hard-cooked eggs, sliced

½ cup pitted ripe olives (optional)

¼ cup sliced green onion (4 medium)

4 anchovy fillets, drained, rinsed, and patted dry (optional)

Fresh chervil (optional)

Time

Preparation	30 min.
Chilling	2 to 24 hrs.

Per Serving

Calories	365
Protein	24 g
Carbohydrate	31 g
Total Fat	17 g
Saturated Fat	3 g
Cholesterol	138 mg
Sodium	254 mg
Potassium	964 mg

Wash green beans; remove ends and strings. In a large covered saucepan or Dutch oven cook green beans and potatoes in boiling water for 15 to 20 minutes or till just tender. Drain; place vegetables in a medium mixing bowl. Cover and chill for 2 to 24 hours.

For dressing, in a screw-top jar combine oil, vinegar, sugar, tarragon, dry mustard, and pepper. Cover and shake well.

To serve, line 4 salad plates with lettuce leaves. Arrange green beans, potatoes, tuna or salmon, tomato, eggs, and olives (if desired) on the lettuce-lined plates. Sprinkle each serving with green onion. Top each salad with an anchovy fillet and garnish with chervil, if desired. Shake dressing well; pour over salads. Makes 4 main-dish servings.

Along the Baltic Sea, cooks refer to fish as a "gift of the sea." This tangy salad features cod, one of their favorite gifts.

BALTIC FISH SALAD

1 pound fresh **or** *frozen skinless cod* **or** *other firm-textured fish fillets, cut into bite-size pieces*

½ cup water

¼ teaspoon salt

1½ cups chopped, seeded cucumber (1 medium)

½ cup dairy sour cream

¼ cup mayonnaise **or** *salad dressing*

2 tablespoons snipped fresh dill **or** *2 teaspoons dried dillweed*

2 tablespoons prepared horseradish

1 teaspoon sugar

¼ teaspoon salt

¼ teaspoon pepper

Lettuce leaves

Fresh dill (optional)

Cucumber slices (optional)

Time

Preparation	20 min.
Chilling	4 to 6 hrs.

Per Serving

Calories	271
Protein	21 g
Carbohydrate	6 g
Total Fat	18 g
Saturated Fat	6 g
Cholesterol	68 mg
Sodium	438 mg
Potassium	439 mg

Thaw fish, if frozen. Measure thickness of fish. In a large skillet combine water and ¼ teaspoon salt; add fish. Bring to boiling; reduce heat. Cover and simmer till fish just flakes with a fork. (Allow 4 to 6 minutes per ½-inch thickness of fish.) Drain fish; set aside.

In a large mixing bowl stir together chopped cucumber, sour cream, mayonnaise or salad dressing, dill, horseradish, sugar, ¼ teaspoon salt, and pepper. Gently stir the fish into the cucumber mixture. Cover and chill for 4 to 6 hours.

To serve, line 4 salad plates with lettuce leaves. Divide fish mixture among plates. Garnish with fresh dill and cucumber slices, if desired. Makes 4 main-dish servings.

POLISH CELERIAC SALAD

1¼ pounds celeriac, peeled and cut into julienne strips (about 3¼ cups)

3 tablespoons olive oil or salad oil

3 tablespoons white wine vinegar or white vinegar

1 tablespoon snipped fresh dill or 1 teaspoon dried dillweed

⅛ teaspoon salt

Dash pepper

2 tablespoons finely chopped onion

In a covered saucepan cook the celeriac in a small amount of boiling water for 6 to 7 minutes or till tender. Drain celeriac.

❧

Meanwhile, for dressing, in a screw-top jar combine olive oil or salad oil, vinegar, dill, salt, and pepper. Cover and shake well.

❧

In a medium mixing bowl combine celeriac and onion. Shake dressing well; pour over celeriac. Cover and chill for 2 to 24 hours, stirring occasionally. Makes 4 side-dish servings.

Resourceful Polish cooks use root vegetables such as celeriac during the winter months when lettuce and other salad vegetables are unavailable.

Time

Preparation	*15 min.*
Chilling	*2 to 24 hrs.*

Per Serving

Calories	*118*
Protein	*1 g*
Carbohydrate	*7 g*
Total Fat	*10 g*
Saturated Fat	*1 g*
Cholesterol	*0 mg*
Sodium	*132 mg*
Potassium	*197 mg*

Traditionally, the beets, potatoes, and cucumbers are marinated and served separately. But to simplify the recipe, we marinated the potatoes and cucumbers in one bowl.

Time

Preparation	1 hr.
Chilling	4 to 24 hrs.

Per Serving

Calories	154
Protein	4 g
Carbohydrate	36 g
Total Fat	2 g
Saturated Fat	0 g
Cholesterol	0 mg
Sodium	85 mg
Potassium	507 mg

GERMAN POTATO, CUCUMBER, AND BEET SALAD

3 medium beets or one 16-ounce can sliced beets

¾ pound whole tiny new potatoes, quartered

1 cup sliced cucumber (1 small)

2 tablespoons snipped chives

1 tablespoon snipped fresh dill or 1 teaspoon dried dillweed

¾ cup vinegar

¼ cup sugar

1 tablespoon coarse-grain brown mustard

1½ teaspoons celery seed

Lettuce leaves

Fresh dill (optional)

For fresh beets, in a large covered saucepan cook whole beets in boiling water for 40 to 50 minutes or till tender; drain. Cool slightly. Slip off skins and slice beets. (*Or,* drain canned beets.) Place beets in a medium mixing bowl; set aside.

Meanwhile, in another large covered saucepan cook potatoes in boiling water for 12 to 15 minutes or till tender; drain. Cool slightly. Place potatoes in a large mixing bowl. Stir in cucumber slices, chives, and dill. Set aside.

For dressing, in a screw-top jar combine vinegar, sugar, mustard, and celery seed. Cover and shake till the sugar dissolves. Pour *¼ cup* of the dressing over the beets; toss lightly to coat. Pour remaining dressing over the potato mixture; toss lightly to coat. Cover and chill both mixtures for 4 to 24 hours, stirring each occasionally.

To serve, line 4 salad plates with lettuce leaves. Using a slotted spoon, remove beets and potato mixture from marinades. Discard beet marinade; reserve potato mixture marinade. On each plate arrange beets, potatoes, and cucumber slices. Stir marinade used for potato mixture; pour marinade over each salad. Garnish with fresh dill, if desired. Makes 4 side-dish servings.

WELSH LEEK SALAD

6 medium leeks

2 cloves garlic, minced

¼ cup salad oil

¼ cup cider vinegar

2 tablespoons water

1 tablespoon snipped fresh tarragon **or** ½ teaspoon dried tarragon, crushed

1 tablespoon snipped parsley

2 teaspoons sugar

1 teaspoon Worcestershire sauce

⅛ teaspoon pepper

2 medium tomatoes, cut into thin wedges

Lettuce leaves

1 hard-cooked egg, chopped

Rinse leeks several times with cold water. Remove any tough outer leaves. Trim roots from base. Cut leeks into ½-inch-thick slices, cutting 1 inch into the green portion. Discard the remaining green portion. In a medium covered saucepan cook leeks and garlic in a small amount of boiling water for 5 minutes or till leeks are crisp-tender; drain. Transfer leeks and garlic to a medium mixing bowl.

❧

For marinade, in a screw-top jar combine oil, vinegar, water, tarragon, parsley, sugar, Worcestershire sauce, and pepper. Cover and shake well. Pour marinade over the leek mixture. Cover and marinate for 2 to 24 hours, stirring occasionally.

❧

To serve, stir tomato wedges into the leek mixture. Line 4 salad plates with lettuce leaves. Using a slotted spoon, transfer leeks and tomatoes from the marinade to the lettuce-lined plates. Sprinkle each salad with hard-cooked egg. Makes 4 side-dish servings.

Rinsing the leeks several times removes the dirt that often gets trapped between the leaves as the leek grows.

Time

Preparation	25 min.
Marinating	2 to 24 hrs.

Per Serving

Calories	201
Protein	3 g
Carbohydrate	15 g
Total Fat	15 g
Saturated Fat	2 g
Cholesterol	53 mg
Sodium	48 mg
Potassium	310 mg

Appetizer Salads

Open your next dinner party with a spectacular first-course salad. Each of these sophisticated salads is artfully arranged, creating an eye-pleasing opener that will complement the rest of your menu.

ASPARAGUS AND TOMATO SALAD

When buying asparagus, look for crisp, thin spears with tightly closed tips.

*¾ pound green **and/or** white asparagus spears*

*¼ cup mayonnaise **or** salad dressing*

1 tablespoon Dijon-style mustard

1 teaspoon vinegar

Dash bottled hot pepper sauce

*Boston **or** Bibb lettuce leaves*

2 hard-cooked eggs, sliced

*6 to 8 red **or** yellow baby pear tomatoes, halved, **or** 2 red **or** yellow plum tomatoes, cut into wedges*

1 cup watercress (optional)

Chive flowers (optional)

Tomatillo wedges (optional)

Snap off and discard woody bases from asparagus. If desired, scrape off scales. Cook asparagus, covered, in a small amount of boiling water for 4 to 8 minutes or till crisp-tender; drain. Place asparagus in a flat container. Cover and chill for 2 to 24 hours.

❦

For dressing, in a small mixing bowl stir together mayonnaise or salad dressing, mustard, vinegar, and bottled hot pepper sauce. Cover and chill for 2 to 24 hours.

❦

To serve, line 4 salad plates with lettuce leaves. Top each with asparagus spears, hard-cooked egg slices, tomatoes, and, if desired, watercress. Pour dressing over each serving. If desired, garnish with chive flowers and tomatillo wedges. Makes 4 servings.

Time

Preparation	25 min.
Chilling	2 to 24 hrs.

Per Serving

Calories	169
Protein	6 g
Carbohydrate	7 g
Total Fat	15 g
Saturated Fat	3 g
Cholesterol	114 mg
Sodium	233 mg
Potassium	349 mg

Dress up your salad with scored cucumber slices. Here's how: Run the tines of a fork lengthwise down a cucumber, pressing to break the skin. Repeat at regular intervals, and then slice the cucumber.

Time

Start to finish 25 min.

Per Serving

Calories	282
Protein	10 g
Carbohydrate	18 g
Total Fat	19 g
Saturated Fat	2 g
Cholesterol	12 mg
Sodium	342 mg
Potassium	345 mg

SMOKED SALMON SALAD WITH LEMON VINAIGRETTE

2 ounces rice sticks, broken

Cooking oil **or** *shortening for deep-fat frying*

4 red-tip leaf lettuce leaves

4 Boston **or** *Bibb lettuce leaves*

4 cups shredded mixed greens

6 ounces thinly sliced smoked salmon (lox)

1 cup sliced cucumber (1 small)

Edible flowers (such as nasturtium, borage, **or** *pansy)*

Lemon Vinaigrette

About 1 hour before serving time, in a 3-quart saucepan or wok heat 1½ to 2 inches of cooking oil to 375°. Fry unsoaked rice sticks, a few at a time, in the hot oil about 5 seconds or till rice sticks puff and rise to the top. Using a wire strainer or slotted spoon, remove rice sticks from oil. Drain on paper towels.

To serve, line 4 salad plates with red-tip and Boston or Bibb lettuce leaves. Top with rice sticks. Arrange shredded greens in the center of each plate. Cut salmon into strips and roll up. Arrange salmon, cucumber slices, and edible flowers on each plate. Shake Lemon Vinaigrette; pour over each serving. Makes 4 servings.

LEMON VINAIGRETTE

In a screw-top jar combine ¼ cup *hazelnut oil, almond oil, or olive oil;* ½ teaspoon finely shredded *lemon peel;* ¼ cup *lemon juice;* 2 teaspoons *sugar;* ½ teaspoon *dry mustard;* and ⅛ teaspoon *pepper.* Cover and shake well. Makes about ½ cup.

Italian Vinaigrette Salad

Using one of our oil-free dressings from page 213 will help cut the fat in this salad.

Lettuce leaves

1 6½-ounce jar marinated artichoke hearts, drained

2 carrots, cut into julienne strips (1 cup)

1 green pepper, cut into julienne strips (1 cup)

4 ounces thinly sliced salami **or** *ham*

1 3½-ounce can tuna (water pack), drained and broken into chunks

½ cup cubed mozzarella **or** *fontina cheese (2 ounces)*

½ cup pitted ripe olives **or** *pimiento-stuffed olives (optional)*

1 2-ounce can anchovy fillets, drained (optional)

Italian Vinaigrette (see recipe, page 211)

Line a large platter with lettuce leaves. Cut any large artichoke hearts in half. Arrange artichoke hearts, carrots, green pepper, salami or ham, tuna, and cheese on the lettuce leaves. Top with olives and anchovy fillets, if desired. Shake Italian Vinaigrette well; pour over salad. Makes 4 servings.

Time

Start to finish   30 min.

Iceberg Ideas

A mild flavor and a crisp texture make iceberg lettuce a popular choice for salad greens. Here are some different ways it can be served in salads.

Shredded: Cut a head of lettuce in half lengthwise. Place each half, cut side down, on a cutting board. Cut the lettuce crosswise into long, coarse shreds.

Rafts: Cut a head of lettuce crosswise into 1-inch-thick slices.

Chunks: Cut lettuce into rafts. Cut each raft crosswise and then lengthwise to get bite-size chunks.

Wedges: Cut a head of lettuce in half lengthwise. Place each half, cut side down, on a cutting board. Cut each half lengthwise into three or four wedges.

Per Serving

Calories	382
Protein	17 g
Carbohydrate	14 g
Total Fat	30 g
Saturated Fat	7 g
Cholesterol	40 mg
Sodium	700 mg
Potassium	439 mg

Walnut oil mingles with sherry in the richly flavored dressing that adorns this sophisticated salad.

APPLE AND WALNUT SALAD

*3 tablespoons walnut oil **or** salad oil*

2 tablespoons white wine vinegar

1 tablespoon dry sherry

⅛ teaspoon pepper

2 medium heads Belgian endive

2 red apples, thinly sliced

¼ cup coarsely chopped walnuts, toasted

¼ cup crumbled blue cheese (1 ounce)

Time

Start to finish   20 min.

Per Serving

Calories	213
Protein	3 g
Carbohydrate	13 g
Total Fat	17 g
Saturated Fat	2 g
Cholesterol	5 mg
Sodium	105 mg
Potassium	196 mg

For dressing, in a screw-top jar combine walnut oil or salad oil, white wine vinegar, sherry, and pepper. Cover and shake well.

Separate leaves of Belgian endive. Arrange leaves on 4 salad plates. Place apple slices on Belgian endive. Sprinkle with walnuts and blue cheese. Shake dressing well; pour over salads. Makes 4 servings.

Keeping Fruit Fresh

The secret to a great fruit salad is luscious, fresh-looking pieces of fruit. To keep fruit such as apples, pears, peaches, apricots, and nectarines from turning brown after it's cut, dip the cut pieces into, or brush them with, lemon juice or a mixture of lemon juice and water. A mixture of ascorbic acid color keeper and water, mixed according to package directions, keeps fruit fresh, too.

FIDDLEHEAD FERN SALAD

16 fiddlehead ferns

3 tablespoons hazelnut oil **or** walnut oil

3 tablespoons raspberry vinegar

1 teaspoon sugar

Red-tip leaf lettuce

1 cup small whole fresh mushrooms

2 tablespoons snipped chives

Edible flowers (such as violets, pansies, **or** borage) (optional)

Wash fiddlehead ferns thoroughly under running water; set aside.

❧

For dressing, in a screw-top jar combine hazelnut oil or walnut oil, raspberry vinegar, and sugar. Cover and shake well.

❧

Line 4 salad plates with lettuce leaves. Arrange fiddlehead ferns and mushrooms atop lettuce. Sprinkle with chives. Shake dressing well; pour over each serving. If desired, garnish with violets, pansies, or borage. Makes 4 servings.

Fiddlehead ferns are the tightly curled, green shoots of certain ferns, such as the ostrich fern, that are available only for a few weeks in the spring.

Time

Start to finish   15 min.

Per Serving

Calories	*116*
Protein	*2 g*
Carbohydrate	*5 g*
Total Fat	*11 g*
Saturated Fat	*1 g*
Cholesterol	*0 mg*
Sodium	*7 mg*
Potassium	*277 mg*

For a simpler salad with the same great flavor, cook one 9-ounce package of frozen artichoke hearts instead of the fresh artichokes. Drain and chill them. Then arrange the salad ingredients on individual plates.

Orange and Avocado-Stuffed Artichokes

4 small artichokes

Lemon juice

Escarole leaves or *curly endive leaves*

3 oranges, peeled and sectioned

1 medium avocado, seeded, peeled, and cut into chunks

½ cup Blue Cheese Dressing (see recipe, page 208)

or Creamy Italian Dressing (see recipe, page 206)

Time

Preparation	35 min.
Chilling	4 to 24 hrs.

Per Serving

Calories	300
Protein	9 g
Carbohydrate	28 g
Total Fat	20 g
Saturated Fat	4 g
Cholesterol	8 mg
Sodium	260 mg
Potassium	918 mg

Wash artichokes; trim stems and remove loose outer leaves. Cut off 1 inch from each top; snip off the sharp leaf tips. Brush the cut edges with a little lemon juice. In a large saucepan or Dutch oven bring a large amount of water to boiling. Add artichokes. Return to boiling; reduce heat. Cover and simmer for 20 to 25 minutes or till a leaf pulls out easily. Drain artichokes upside down on paper towels. Spread leaves apart. Pull out center leaves and scrape out choke with a spoon; discard choke. Cover artichokes and chill for 4 to 24 hours.

To serve, line 4 salad plates with lettuce leaves. Place an artichoke on each. Spoon some of the orange sections and avocado chunks into the center of each artichoke. Pour Blue Cheese Dressing or Creamy Italian Dressing over each artichoke. Makes 4 servings.

HEARTS OF PALM SALAD

Hearts of palm are the edible interiors of young palm trees. Look for them in the canned fruit and vegetable aisle of your supermarket.

1 14-ounce can hearts of palm, drained

3 tablespoons salad oil

3 tablespoons white wine vinegar or white vinegar

1 tablespoon water

1 teaspoon snipped fresh oregano or ¼ teaspoon dried oregano, crushed

1 teaspoon snipped fresh savory or ¼ teaspoon dried savory, crushed

5 cups torn Boston or Bibb lettuce

1 cup torn radicchio or shredded red cabbage

⅓ cup shredded carrot (1 small)

Fresh oregano or savory (optional)

Cut the hearts of palm into ¼-inch-thick slices; chill till serving time.

❧

For dressing, in a screw-top jar combine salad oil, vinegar, water, oregano, and savory. Cover and shake well.

❧

In a large mixing bowl combine Boston or Bibb lettuce, raddichio or red cabbage, and carrot. Toss lightly to mix.

❧

To serve, arrange lettuce mixture on 6 salad plates. Top with hearts of palm. Shake dressing well; pour over each serving. Garnish with oregano or savory, if desired. Makes 6 servings.

Time

Start to finish   25 min.

Per Serving

Calories	95
Protein	3 g
Carbohydrate	6 g
Total Fat	7 g
Saturated Fat	1 g
Cholesterol	0 mg
Sodium	7 mg
Potassium	271 mg

Two Oriental mushrooms join forces in this distinctive salad. The dried mushrooms have a chewy texture and the enoki mushrooms have a delicate flavor and crisp texture.

MIXED MUSHROOM SALAD

4 dried mushrooms

2 tablespoons olive oil or salad oil

1 tablespoon balsamic vinegar or white wine vinegar

1 tablespoon water

3 ounces enoki mushrooms (about 1 cup)

1 tablespoon sliced lemongrass (1 stalk) or ½ teaspoon finely shredded lemon peel

4 cups mesclun or 2 cups torn mixed greens and 2 cups torn curly endive

Fiddlehead ferns (optional)

Edible flowers (such as dianthus or borage) (optional)

Enoki mushrooms (optional)

In a small mixing bowl soak the dried mushrooms for 30 minutes in enough warm water to cover. Rinse mushrooms well and squeeze to drain thoroughly. Slice the mushrooms thinly, discarding the stems; set mushrooms aside.

❦

For dressing, in a screw-top jar combine olive oil or salad oil, balsamic vinegar or white wine vinegar, and water. Cover and shake well.

❦

In a medium mixing bowl combine dried mushroom slices, the 3 ounces enoki mushrooms, and lemongrass or lemon peel. Toss lightly to mix. Line 4 salad plates with mesclun. Spoon mushroom mixture atop mesclun. Shake dressing well; pour over each serving. If desired, garnish with fiddlehead ferns, edible flowers, and additional enoki mushrooms. Serves 4.

Time

Start to finish 40 min.

Per Serving

Calories	84
Protein	1 g
Carbohydrate	5 g
Total Fat	7 g
Saturated Fat	1 g
Cholesterol	0 mg
Sodium	6 mg
Potassium	201 mg

Use 12 ounces of shrimp and this colorful salad becomes a luncheon or dinner entrée.

SHRIMP WITH LIME-SOY VINAIGRETTE

½ pound fresh or frozen peeled and deveined medium shrimp (about 12)

12 baby carrots

1½ cups pea pods (about 4 ounces)

4 Boston or Bibb lettuce leaves

Lime-Soy Vinaigrette

Bring 4 cups *water* and 1 teaspoon *salt* to boiling. Add shrimp. Simmer, uncovered, for 1 to 3 minutes or till shrimp turn pink, stirring occasionally. Drain shrimp and rinse under cold running water. Cover and chill shrimp for 2 to 24 hours.

In a medium covered saucepan cook carrots in a small amount of boiling water for 8 minutes. Add pea pods and cook about 2 minutes more or till carrots and pea pods are crisp-tender. Drain carrots and pea pods. Cover and chill carrots and pea pods for 2 to 24 hours.

To serve, line 4 salad plates with lettuce leaves. Arrange shrimp, carrots, and pea pods on the lettuce-lined plates. Shake Lime-Soy Vinaigrette; pour over each serving. Makes 4 servings.

LIME-SOY VINAIGRETTE

In a screw-top jar combine 2 tablespoons *salad oil*, ½ teaspoon finely shredded *lime peel*, 2 tablespoons *lime juice*, 1 tablespoon *soy sauce*, 2 teaspoons *honey*, and a dash ground *red pepper.* Cover and shake well. Makes about ⅓ cup.

Time

Preparation	20 min.
Chilling	2 to 24 hrs.

Per Serving

Calories	159
Protein	12 g
Carbohydrate	13 g
Total Fat	7 g
Saturated Fat	1 g
Cholesterol	83 mg
Sodium	903 mg
Potassium	343 mg

VEGETABLE MEDLEY SALAD

*S*et the stage for an elegant meal with this vegetable trio—julienne carrot strips, enoki mushrooms, and pea pods.

¾ cup pea pods (about 2 ounces)

*2 cups mesclun **or** torn radicchio*

1 cup torn curly endive

1 cup torn red-tip leaf lettuce

4 ounces enoki mushrooms (about 1½ cups)

2 carrots, cut into julienne strips (1 cup)

½ cup Green Goddess Dressing (see recipe, page 207)

In a medium covered saucepan cook pea pods in a small amount of boiling water about 2 minutes or till crisp-tender. Drain pea pods and rinse with cold water. Set aside.

In a large mixing bowl toss together mesclun or radicchio, curly endive, and red-tip leaf lettuce. Arrange the mixed greens on 4 salad plates. Top with pea pods, enoki mushrooms, and carrots. Pour Green Goddess Dressing over each serving. Makes 4 servings.

Time

Start to finish   25 min.

Cool Down

Most salads taste best when served refreshingly cold. Try one of these cooling tips when you want to serve a well-chilled salad.
- Chill ingredients thoroughly before you make the salad.
- Prepare the salad but do not add the dressing. Cover the salad and chill it for at least 1 hour before serving.
- For a quick cool down, cover the salad and place it in the freezer for 20 minutes.

Per Serving

Calories	132
Protein	3 g
Carbohydrate	10 g
Total Fat	10 g
Saturated Fat	2 g
Cholesterol	10 mg
Sodium	101 mg
Potassium	465 mg

PAPAYA AND AVOCADO SALAD

2 tablespoons salad oil

2 tablespoons lime juice **or** *lemon juice*

2 teaspoons sugar

⅛ teaspoon ground cumin

Several dashes bottled hot pepper sauce

Lettuce leaves

1 medium papaya, seeded, peeled, and sliced

1 medium avocado, seeded, peeled, and sliced

1 medium carambola (star fruit), sliced

1 tablespoon snipped fresh cilantro **or** *parsley*

8 to 12 sprigs watercress (optional)

For dressing, in a screw-top jar combine salad oil, lime juice or lemon juice, sugar, cumin, and hot pepper sauce. Cover and shake well.

❦

Line 4 salad plates with lettuce leaves. Alternate papaya and avocado slices on each lettuce-lined plate. Add carambola slices to each plate. Sprinkle with cilantro or parsley. If desired, garnish with watercress. Shake dressing well; pour over each salad. Makes 4 servings.

When buying papayas, look for those on which at least two-thirds of the skin is yellow. A ripe papaya yields slightly to gentle pressure. Slightly green papayas will ripen at room temperature in three to five days.

Time

Start to finish   20 min.

Per Serving

Calories	194
Protein	2 g
Carbohydrate	17 g
Total Fat	15 g
Saturated Fat	2 g
Cholesterol	0 mg
Sodium	10 mg
Potassium	591 mg

ORIENTAL SESAME-NOODLE SALAD

You'll find soba, a Japanese pasta, in Oriental and specialty food stores.

2 ounces buckwheat noodles (soba) or whole wheat spaghetti, broken

1 small yellow summer squash or zucchini, halved lengthwise and sliced (1 cup)

½ cup halved cherry tomatoes

¼ cup fresh bean sprouts

4 teaspoons soy sauce

1 tablespoon rice vinegar or white vinegar

¼ teaspoon grated gingerroot

¼ teaspoon roasted sesame oil

Dash bottled hot pepper sauce

3 cups spinach leaves

1 tablespoon sliced green onion (optional)

1 teaspoon sesame seed, toasted (optional)

In a large saucepan cook the buckwheat noodles or spaghetti according to the package directions. Before draining the pasta, stir in the summer squash or zucchini and cherry tomatoes. Then drain immediately. Rinse the noodle and vegetable mixture under cold water; drain well. Return mixture to the saucepan. Stir in the bean sprouts.

Meanwhile, for dressing, in a small mixing bowl combine the soy sauce, vinegar, gingerroot, sesame oil, and hot pepper sauce. Toss with the drained noodle and vegetable mixture.

Arrange spinach on a large platter or 4 salad plates. Top with noodle and vegetable mixture. If desired, sprinkle with sliced green onion and sesame seed. Makes 4 servings.

Time

Start to finish   25 min.

Per Serving

Calories	96
Protein	5 g
Carbohydrate	17 g
Total Fat	2 g
Saturated Fat	0 g
Cholesterol	26 mg
Sodium	452 mg
Potassium	434 mg

Main-Dish Salads

Today's main-dish salads are much more than a basic Chef's Salad. They have an exciting and delicious new look. Some bring together stir-fried meat and fresh greens, such as Marinated Steak Salad with Shiitake Mushrooms. Others, such as Shrimp Salad with Berry Vinaigrette, are masterfully arranged to create an entrée as pleasant to view as it is to eat. Turn the page and select one of our bold and hearty main-dish salads. It's sure to hit the spot.

LAMB BROCHETTE SALAD

1 pound lean boneless lamb **or** *boneless beef top round steak*

½ cup olive oil **or** *salad oil*

½ cup lemon juice

2 cloves garlic, minced

2 teaspoons ground cumin

1 teaspoon ground cinnamon

1 teaspoon paprika

¼ teaspoon crushed red pepper

4 ounces chèvre (goat's cheese)

Leaf lettuce leaves

1 15-ounce can garbanzo beans, chilled and drained

2 small tomatoes, cut into wedges

1 cup thinly sliced cucumber (1 small)

Fresh cilantro (optional)

Stick cinnamon (optional)

A *spicy marinade, which doubles as the dressing, gives a wonderfully exotic flavor to this imaginative salad.*

Trim fat from lamb or beef. Partially freeze meat. Thinly slice across the grain into bite-size strips. Place meat in a mixing bowl.

※

For marinade, in a screw-top jar combine oil, lemon juice, garlic, cumin, cinnamon, paprika, and red pepper. Cover and shake well. Pour *half* of the marinade over the meat, reserving remaining marinade for dressing. Marinate the meat at room temperature for 15 minutes.

※

Meanwhile, shape the chèvre into 12 small balls. Place the cheese balls in a flat container. Cover and chill.

※

To prepare lamb skewers, drain meat, discarding marinade. On 8 long or 16 short skewers, loosely thread meat accordion-style. Place skewers on the unheated rack of a broiler pan. Broil 3 to 4 inches from the heat for 4 to 5 minutes or to desired doneness, turning once.

※

Meanwhile, line 4 salad plates with lettuce leaves. Arrange cheese balls, garbanzo beans, tomato wedges, and cucumber slices on the lettuce. Divide the skewers among the plates. Shake reserved marinade; pour over each serving. If desired, garnish with cilantro and stick cinnamon. Makes 4 servings.

Time

Start to finish   70 min.

Per Serving

Calories	*464*
Protein	*32 g*
Carbohydrate	*27 g*
Total Fat	*26 g*
Saturated Fat	*4 g*
Cholesterol	*85 mg*
Sodium	*183 mg*
Potassium	*713 mg*

Roll cutting gives carrots a triangular shape. To roll-cut a carrot, hold a sharp knife at a 45-degree angle to the carrot. Make the first cut, then give the carrot a quarter- to half-turn and angle-cut again.

BEEF SALAD STIR-FRY

¾ pound beef top round steak

1 cup roll-cut carrots (3 small)

1 tablespoon salad oil

1 cup sliced yellow summer squash **or** *zucchini (1 small)*

4 green onions, cut into 2-inch pieces (½ cup)

3 cups torn leaf lettuce

2 cups torn curly endive **or** *escarole*

½ cup Dijon Dressing (see recipe, page 206)

Trim fat from beef. Partially freeze the beef. Thinly slice across the grain into bite-size strips. Set meat aside.

❧

In a medium covered saucepan cook carrots in a small amount of boiling water for 3 minutes. Drain carrots; set aside.

❧

Pour oil into a wok or large skillet. (Add more oil as necessary during cooking.) Preheat over medium-high heat. Add the carrots and squash or zucchini; stir-fry for 1½ minutes. Add the green onions; stir-fry for 1½ to 2 minutes more or till vegetables are crisp-tender. Remove the vegetables from the wok. Add beef to the hot wok; stir-fry for 2 to 3 minutes or to desired doneness. Remove beef from the wok.

❧

In a large salad bowl toss together lettuce and curly endive or escarole. Add stir-fried vegetables and beef. Toss lightly to mix. Pour Dijon Dressing over salad. Toss lightly to coat. Makes 4 servings.

Time

Start to finish   50 min.

Per Serving

Calories	240
Protein	24 g
Carbohydrate	12 g
Total Fat	12 g
Saturated Fat	4 g
Cholesterol	63 mg
Sodium	165 mg
Potassium	763 mg

BEEF SALAD WITH FRESH BASIL DRESSING

6 cups torn mixed greens

½ pound lean cooked beef, cut into thin strips (1½ cups)

½ cup thinly sliced parsnip (1 small)

½ cup thinly sliced carrot (1 medium)

½ cup sliced zucchini (½ of a medium)

½ cup broccoli flowerets

Fresh Basil Dressing

½ of a 16-ounce can julienne beets, well drained

In a large salad bowl combine greens, beef, parsnip, carrot, zucchini, and broccoli flowerets. Toss lightly to mix. Pour Fresh Basil Dressing over salad. Toss lightly to coat. Top with drained beets. Makes 4 servings.

FRESH BASIL DRESSING

In a small mixing bowl stir together ½ cup *buttermilk;* 3 tablespoons *mayonnaise or salad dressing;* 1 tablespoon snipped fresh *basil or* 1 teaspoon dried *basil,* crushed; 1 tablespoon *lemon juice;* 1 teaspoon *sugar;* and dash *pepper.* Cover and store in the refrigerator for up to 2 weeks. Makes about ¾ cup.

When buying parsnips, select small, evenly shaped ones. Large parsnips will be tough.

Time

Start to finish   30 min.

Per Serving

Calories	*255*
Protein	*20 g*
Carbohydrate	*13 g*
Total Fat	*14 g*
Saturated Fat	*4 g*
Cholesterol	*51 mg*
Sodium	*235 mg*
Potassium	*724 mg*

MARINATED STEAK SALAD WITH SHIITAKE MUSHROOMS

Shiitake mushrooms add a rich, delicate flavor to the bed of greens. If you have difficulty locating them, substitute canned straw mushrooms or other mushrooms.

¾ pound boneless beef sirloin steak

½ cup olive oil or salad oil

½ cup wine vinegar

2 tablespoons dry sherry

2 tablespoons soy sauce

1 tablespoon brown sugar

1 clove garlic, minced

⅛ teaspoon ground ginger

12 cups torn mixed greens

1½ cups sliced fresh shiitake mushrooms

½ cup sliced green onion (8 medium)

1 tablespoon olive oil or salad oil

1 large sweet red or green pepper, cut into thin strips

Time

Preparation	35 min.
Marinating	6 to 24 hrs.
Assembling	25 min.

Per Serving

Calories	327
Protein	16 g
Carbohydrate	13 g
Total Fat	23 g
Saturated Fat	4 g
Cholesterol	38 mg
Sodium	393 mg
Potassium	564 mg

Trim fat from beef. Partially freeze the beef. Thinly slice across the grain into bite-size strips. Place meat in a deep bowl.

❧

For marinade, in a screw-top jar combine the ½ cup oil, vinegar, sherry, soy sauce, brown sugar, garlic, and ginger. Cover and shake well. Pour marinade over meat. Marinate in the refrigerator for 6 to 24 hours, stirring occasionally.

❧

To serve, in a large mixing bowl toss together greens, shiitake mushrooms, and green onion. Divide the mixture among 6 salad plates; set aside.

❧

Drain meat, reserving ⅔ cup marinade. Pour the 1 tablespoon oil into a wok or large skillet. (Add more oil as necessary during cooking.) Preheat over medium-high heat. Add pepper strips; stir-fry for 2 minutes or till crisp-tender. Remove pepper strips from the wok.

❧

Add meat to the wok; stir-fry for 2 to 3 minutes or to desired doneness. Return pepper strips to the wok; push meat and pepper strips from the center of the wok. Add reserved marinade to the center of the wok. Cook and stir till bubbly. Stir all the ingredients in the wok together. Divide the hot meat mixture among the salad plates. Serve immediately. Makes 6 servings.

BEEF AND BROCCOLI SALAD

Crunchy chow mein noodles create a tasty topping for this easy tossed salad.

¼ *cup salad oil*

¼ *cup rice vinegar* **or** *white wine vinegar*

2 tablespoons soy sauce

1 tablespoon sugar

⅛ *teaspoon five-spice powder* **or** *ground ginger*

3 cups torn romaine

2 cups torn Boston **or** *Bibb lettuce*

2 cups broccoli flowerets

½ *pound lean cooked beef, cut into thin strips (1½ cups)*

1 cup sliced fresh mushrooms

½ *of a 3-ounce can (1 cup) chow mein noodles*

For dressing, in a screw-top jar combine oil, vinegar, soy sauce, sugar, and five-spice powder or ginger. Cover and shake well.

⚜

In a large salad bowl combine romaine, Boston or Bibb lettuce, broccoli flowerets, beef strips, and sliced mushrooms. Shake dressing well; pour over salad. Toss lightly to coat. Sprinkle with chow mein noodles. Makes 4 servings.

Time

Start to finish   25 min.

Per Serving

Calories	309
Protein	20 g
Carbohydrate	12 g
Total Fat	21 g
Saturated Fat	4 g
Cholesterol	43 mg
Sodium	595 mg
Potassium	649 mg

Beef and Potato Salad With Horseradish Dressing

On another occasion, serve this zippy horseradish dressing with hot roast beef or baked ham.

¾ pound baby carrots or one 10-ounce package frozen tiny whole carrots
½ pound whole tiny new potatoes, halved
½ cup dairy sour cream
1 tablespoon prepared horseradish
1 teaspoon milk
Boston or Bibb lettuce leaves
½ pound lean cooked beef, cut into thin strips (1½ cups)
8 radish accordions
4 onion brushes
Cracked black pepper

In a covered saucepan cook fresh carrots and potatoes in boiling water for 12 to 15 minutes or till tender. (*Or,* cook frozen carrots according to package directions.) Drain; transfer carrots and potatoes to a bowl. Cover and chill for 4 to 24 hours.

꧁

For dressing, in a small bowl combine sour cream, horseradish, and the 1 teaspoon milk. Cover; chill 4 to 24 hours. (Before serving, if necessary, stir in additional milk to moisten.)

꧁

Line 4 salad plates with lettuce leaves. Arrange carrots, potatoes, beef, radish accordions, and onion brushes on lettuce-lined plates. Place a dollop of dressing on each serving. Sprinkle each salad with cracked black pepper. Makes 4 servings.

Radish Accordions

For each radish accordion, select a long, narrow radish and make 8 to 10 crosswise cuts ⅛ inch apart, cutting only partially through the radish. Place the radish in ice water about 20 minutes or till the slices fan out.

Onion Brushes

For each onion brush, slice off the roots from a green onion. Remove all but 2 inches of the green portion. Thinly slash both ends of the onion piece to create fringe. Place the onion piece in ice water about 20 minutes or till ends curl.

Time

Preparation	30 min.
Chilling	4 to 24 hrs.

Per Serving

Calories	279
Protein	20 g
Carbohydrate	25 g
Total Fat	11 g
Saturated Fat	6 g
Cholesterol	56 mg
Sodium	95 mg
Potassium	865 mg

Sirloin Salad

¾ *pound boneless beef sirloin steak, cut 1 inch thick*

¼ *cup salad oil*

¼ *cup red wine vinegar*

1 tablespoon snipped fresh thyme **or** *1 teaspoon dried thyme, crushed*

1 tablespoon Dijon-style mustard

¼ *teaspoon coarsely ground pepper*

1½ cups fresh pea pods **or** *one 6-ounce package frozen pea pods, thawed*

2 small carrots

3 cups torn romaine **or** *leaf lettuce*

3 cups torn curly endive **or** *escarole*

8 cherry tomatoes, halved

¼ *cup finely shredded Parmesan cheese*

This salad is a light, refreshing twist on a steak dinner.

Slash fat edges of steak at 1-inch intervals, being careful not to cut into the meat. Place the steak on the unheated rack of a broiler pan. Broil 3 inches from the heat for 6 minutes. Turn steak. Broil to desired doneness (allow 6 to 8 minutes more for medium). Cool slightly; cut into thin slices. Place meat in a deep bowl.

❧

For marinade, in a screw-top jar combine oil, vinegar, thyme, mustard, and pepper. Cover and shake well. Pour marinade over meat. Cover and marinate in the refrigerator for 6 to 24 hours, stirring occasionally.

❧

In a medium covered saucepan cook the fresh pea pods in a small amount of boiling water for 1 to 2 minutes or till crisp-tender. *Do not cook frozen pea pods.* Drain cooked pea pods; rinse with cold water. Set aside.

❧

Use a sharp knife to cut off the ends of each carrot. Cut the carrots into 3-inch pieces; cut each piece lengthwise in half. Use a vegetable peeler to shave each half into thin rectangular slices.

❧

In a large salad bowl combine romaine or leaf lettuce and curly endive or escarole. Add steak and marinade, pea pods, carrots, and cherry tomatoes. Toss lightly to mix. Sprinkle with Parmesan cheese. Makes 4 servings.

Time

Preparation	*30 min.*
Marinating	*6 to 24 hrs.*
Assembling	*20 min.*

Per Serving

Calories	*331*
Protein	*26 g*
Carbohydrate	*13 g*
Total Fat	*21 g*
Saturated Fat	*5 g*
Cholesterol	*61 mg*
Sodium	*285 mg*
Potassium	*776 mg*

Give this stick-to-the-ribs pasta salad an Italian flavor by switching the cheddar cheese to provolone or mozzarella.

BEEF AND VEGETABLE PASTA SALAD

1⅓ cups cavatelli (4 ounces)

2 small zucchini, halved lengthwise and sliced (2 cups)

½ pound lean cooked beef or pork, cut into thin strips (1½ cups)

1 6½-ounce jar marinated artichoke hearts, drained and quartered

½ cup cubed cheddar or Colby cheese (2 ounces)

½ cup chopped sweet red and/or green pepper (1 small)

½ cup mayonnaise or salad dressing

2 tablespoons snipped parsley

2 tablespoons snipped fresh basil or 1 teaspoon dried basil, crushed

1 tablespoon white wine vinegar or white vinegar

¼ teaspoon pepper

Several dashes bottled hot pepper sauce

Curly endive or lettuce leaves

8 cherry tomatoes, halved

Time

| Preparation | 30 min. |
| Chilling | 4 to 24 hrs. |

Per Serving

Calories	527
Protein	28 g
Carbohydrate	31 g
Total Fat	34 g
Saturated Fat	8 g
Cholesterol	79 mg
Sodium	516 mg
Potassium	660 mg

Cook pasta according to package directions. Drain pasta. Rinse with *cold* water; drain again.

In a large mixing bowl combine pasta, sliced zucchini, beef or pork strips, artichoke hearts, cubed cheese, and chopped pepper.

For dressing, in a small mixing bowl stir together mayonnaise or salad dressing, parsley, basil, vinegar, pepper, and hot pepper sauce. Pour dressing over the pasta mixture. Toss lightly to coat. Cover and chill for 4 to 24 hours.

To serve, line 4 salad plates with curly endive or lettuce leaves. Stir tomatoes into pasta mixture. Divide pasta mixture among plates. Makes 4 servings.

For a fat-trimmed version of this beef salad, use fat-free mayonnaise or salad·dressing and skip the avocado and the olives. You'll cut the fat content by about 18 grams per serving.

Time

Start to finish   30 min.

Per Serving

Calories	455
Protein	23 g
Carbohydrate	11 g
Total Fat	37 g
Saturated Fat	11 g
Cholesterol	74 mg
Sodium	473 mg
Potassium	814 mg

TOSSED BEEF SALAD WITH SALSA DRESSING

4 cups torn mixed greens

½ pound lean cooked beef or pork, cut into bite-size pieces (1½ cups)

1 cup coarsely chopped tomatoes (2 medium)

1 cup shredded cheddar cheese (4 ounces)

1 medium avocado, seeded, peeled, and cut into bite-size pieces

¼ cup sliced green onion (4 medium)

¼ cup sliced pitted ripe olives

Salsa Dressing

In a large salad bowl combine torn mixed greens, beef or pork pieces, chopped tomatoes, cheddar cheese, avocado pieces, green onion, and ripe olives. Toss lightly to mix. Pour Salsa Dressing over salad. Toss lightly to coat. Makes 4 servings.

SALSA DRESSING

In a small mixing bowl stir together ⅓ cup *plain yogurt,* ⅓ cup *mayonnaise or salad dressing,* and 3 tablespoons *salsa.* Cover and store in the refrigerator up to 1 week. Makes about ¾ cup.

BEEF AND VEGETABLE TOSS

In a hurry? Buy the beef from a deli and the cauliflower flowerets from a supermarket salad bar.

1 cup frozen whole kernel corn
4 cups torn leaf lettuce
½ pound cooked lean beef, cut into bite-size strips (1½ cups)
1 cup sliced cauliflower flowerets
1 cup sliced zucchini (1 medium)
1 cup shredded red cabbage
¾ cup Thousand Island Dressing (see recipe, page 205) or desired creamy dressing
1 cup Italian Croutons (see recipe, page 231) or croutons

Cook the frozen corn according to package directions. Drain corn well.

❧

In a large salad bowl combine corn, lettuce, beef strips, cauliflower, zucchini, and red cabbage. Pour Thousand Island Dressing or desired creamy dressing over salad. Toss lightly to coat. Sprinkle with croutons. Makes 4 servings.

The Cutting of Cauliflower
Thinly sliced cauliflower looks delicate and lacey and is easier to manage on a fork than chunky flowerets. To slice cauliflower easily, rinse it under cold running water. Use a paring knife to remove any brown spots. Cut or break the cauliflower into flowerets. Then, thinly slice the flowerets.

Time
Start to finish   25 min.

Per Serving

Calories	421
Protein	22 g
Carbohydrate	22 g
Total Fat	29 g
Saturated Fat	6 g
Cholesterol	86 mg
Sodium	471 mg
Potassium	708 mg

Dress up last night's roast beef with apples, carrot, jicama, and an apple vinaigrette dressing.

Time

Start to finish   20 min.

Per Serving

Calories	345
Protein	18 g
Carbohydrate	27 g
Total Fat	19 g
Saturated Fat	4 g
Cholesterol	43 mg
Sodium	59 mg
Potassium	605 mg

BEEF AND APPLE SALAD

¼ cup apple juice

¼ cup salad oil

2 tablespoons red wine vinegar

Lettuce leaves

½ pound lean cooked beef, cut into thin strips (1½ cups)

2 medium apples, cored and cut into thin wedges

1 cup jicama cut into julienne strips **or** one 8-ounce can sliced water chestnuts, drained

2 medium carrots, cut into julienne strips (1 cup)

¼ cup raisins

For dressing, in a screw-top jar combine apple juice, salad oil, and red wine vinegar. Cover and shake well.

❦

Line 4 salad plates with lettuce. Arrange sliced beef, apple wedges, jicama or water chestnuts, and carrot strips on the lettuce-lined plates. Sprinkle each serving with raisins. Shake dressing well; pour over each serving. Makes 4 servings.

MINTED HAM SALAD

1 8-ounce carton plain yogurt

1 tablespoon snipped fresh mint **or** *1 teaspoon dried mint, crushed*

1 tablespoon milk

2 teaspoons horseradish mustard

⅛ teaspoon onion powder

3 cups assorted cut-up fresh vegetables (sliced zucchini, cauliflower flowerets, broccoli flowerets, and/or sliced carrot)

½ pound cubed lean fully cooked ham (1½ cups)

½ cup shredded cheddar cheese (2 ounces)

Fresh mint (optional)

For dressing, in a small mixing bowl stir together yogurt, mint, milk, horseradish mustard, and onion powder.

☙

In a large mixing bowl combine assorted vegetables, ham, and cheese. Pour dressing over salad. Toss lightly to coat. Serve immediately or cover and chill for 4 to 24 hours. Garnish with fresh mint, if desired. Makes 4 servings.

*N*ext time, add fresh snipped basil in place of the mint.

Time

Start to finish   25 min.

Per Serving

Calories	*202*
Protein	*23 g*
Carbohydrate	*8 g*
Total Fat	*9 g*
Saturated Fat	*5 g*
Cholesterol	*50 mg*
Sodium	*895 mg*
Potassium	*594 mg*

This spicy pork curry becomes a salad when you toss it with Chinese cabbage.

HOT CURRIED PORK SALAD

¾ pound lean boneless pork

3 tablespoons salad oil

3 tablespoons vinegar

1 tablespoon curry powder

1 teaspoon snipped fresh thyme **or** *¼ teaspoon dried thyme, crushed*

1 clove garlic, minced

1 cup bias-sliced celery (2 stalks)

1 medium onion, cut into thin wedges

8 cherry tomatoes, halved

½ cup peanuts

½ cup raisins

4 cups coarsely chopped Chinese cabbage

Time

Start to finish	45 min.

Per Serving

Calories	411
Protein	27 g
Carbohydrate	28 g
Total Fat	25 g
Saturated Fat	4 g
Cholesterol	50 mg
Sodium	162 mg
Potassium	905 mg

Trim fat from pork. Partially freeze the pork. Thinly slice across the grain into bite-size pieces. Set pork aside.

❧

For dressing, in a screw-top jar combine *2 tablespoons* of the oil, the vinegar, curry powder, and thyme. Cover and shake well.

❧

Pour the remaining 1 tablespoon oil into a wok or large skillet. (Add more oil as necessary during cooking). Preheat over medium-high heat. Add garlic; stir-fry for 15 seconds. Add celery and onion; stir-fry about 3 minutes or till vegetables are crisp-tender. Remove vegetables from the wok.

❧

Add the pork to the wok; stir-fry about 3 minutes or till no longer pink. Return vegetables to the wok. Shake dressing well. Stir dressing, tomatoes, peanuts, and raisins into pork mixture and heat through.

❧

Place Chinese cabbage in a large salad bowl. Pour pork mixture over the cabbage. Toss lightly to mix. Makes 4 servings.

HAM AND FRUIT SALAD WITH HONEY-MUSTARD VINAIGRETTE

½ pound thinly sliced, lean, fully cooked ham

8 ounces thinly sliced Monterey Jack cheese or Muenster cheese

Lettuce leaves

2 cups sliced, peeled peaches or frozen peach slices, thawed

2 kiwi fruit, peeled and sliced

1 cup seedless grapes, halved

Honey-Mustard Vinaigrette

Roll up each slice of ham and each slice of cheese. Line 4 salad plates with lettuce leaves. Arrange ham, cheese, peach slices, kiwi fruit, and grapes on the lettuce-lined plates. Shake Honey-Mustard Dressing well; pour over each serving. Makes 4 servings.

HONEY-MUSTARD VINAIGRETTE

In a screw-top jar combine ¼ cup *salad oil,* ¼ cup *vinegar,* 1 tablespoon *honey,* ¼ teaspoon *dry mustard,* and ⅛ teaspoon *pepper.* Cover and shake well. Makes about ½ cup.

Serve this spicy-sweet salad with freshly baked muffins for a scrumptious brunch.

Time

Start to finish   25 min.

Per Serving

Calories	*508*
Protein	*26 g*
Carbohydrate	*29 g*
Total Fat	*34 g*
Saturated Fat	*13 g*
Cholesterol	*73 mg*
Sodium	*873 mg*
Potassium	*600 mg*

This hearty salad makes the most of just-picked summertime vegetables. Look for the peppers, greens, and tomatoes at a farmers' market. Or, use those found in your own garden.

Time

Start to finish   55 min.

Per Serving

Calories	312
Protein	20 g
Carbohydrate	11 g
Total Fat	23 g
Saturated Fat	4 g
Cholesterol	44 mg
Sodium	191 mg
Potassium	629 mg

PORK AND ROASTED PEPPER SALAD

1 medium green pepper

1 medium sweet red pepper

1 medium sweet yellow pepper

⅓ cup olive oil or salad oil

⅓ cup white wine vinegar or white vinegar

1 tablespoon sugar (optional)

1 tablespoon snipped fresh basil or 1 teaspoon dried basil, crushed

¼ teaspoon salt

⅛ teaspoon pepper

4 cups torn mixed greens

½ pound cubed cooked lean pork (1½ cups)

2 medium tomatoes, sliced

1 medium red onion, sliced and separated into rings

Yellow baby pear tomatoes (optional)

Fresh basil (optional)

Red pearl onions (optional)

To roast peppers, quarter the peppers lengthwise. Remove the stems and seeds. Cut small slits into the ends of the pepper pieces to make them lie flat. Place pepper pieces, cut sides down, on a foil-lined baking sheet. Bake in a 425° oven for 20 to 25 minutes or till skins are bubbly and brown. Immediately place pepper pieces in a clean brown paper bag. Close bag tightly; cool.

Meanwhile, for dressing, in a screw-top jar combine oil, vinegar, sugar (if desired), basil, salt, and pepper. Cover and shake well.

Peel the cooled pepper pieces with a sharp knife. Cut lengthwise into ½-inch-wide strips.

Arrange the mixed greens on 4 salad plates. Arrange pepper strips, pork, tomato slices, and onion slices atop greens. Shake dressing well; pour dressing over each serving. If desired, garnish with baby pear tomatoes, fresh basil, and red pearl onions. Makes 4 servings.

Here's a make-ahead tip: Cut up the fresh fruit and prepare the creamy ginger dressing the night before.

Time

Start to finish   30 min.

Per Serving

Calories	416
Protein	16 g
Carbohydrate	20 g
Total Fat	33 g
Saturated Fat	5 g
Cholesterol	45 mg
Sodium	994 mg
Potassium	595 mg

HAM AND MELON SALAD

½ cup mayonnaise **or** *salad dressing*

1 tablespoon Dijon-style mustard

1 teaspoon grated gingerroot **or** *½ teaspoon ground ginger*

2 cups cubed honeydew melon **or** *cantaloupe*

½ pound lean fully cooked ham, cut into bite-size strips (1½ cups)

1½ cups cubed fresh pineapple **or** *one 8-ounce can pineapple chunks (juice pack), drained*

½ cup sliced celery (1 stalk)

⅓ cup coarsely chopped pecans

Lettuce leaves

For dressing, in a small mixing bowl stir together mayonnaise or salad dressing, mustard, and gingerroot or ground ginger. Set dressing aside.

❦

In a large mixing bowl combine honeydew melon or cantaloupe, ham, pineapple, celery, and pecans. Pour dressing over ham mixture. Toss lightly to coat.

❦

Line 4 salad plates with lettuce leaves. Divide the ham mixture among the lettuce-lined plates. Makes 4 servings.

HAM AND CHEESE PASTA SALAD

The ridges of the corkscrew macaroni trap the tarragon vinaigrette, giving this one-dish meal an extra flavor boost.

1½ cups corkscrew macaroni (4 ounces)

½ pound lean fully cooked ham, beef, or turkey, cut into bite-size strips (1½ cups)

1 cup cubed Swiss cheese (4 ounces)

1 cup sliced cauliflower flowerets

½ cup shredded carrot (1 medium)

2 tablespoons snipped chives

¼ cup salad oil

¼ cup tarragon vinegar

1 tablespoon snipped fresh tarragon or 1 teaspoon dried tarragon, crushed

½ teaspoon garlic powder

¼ teaspoon pepper

Lettuce leaves

Cook pasta according to package directions. Drain pasta. Rinse with *cold* water; drain again.

In a large mixing bowl combine pasta; ham, beef, or turkey; Swiss cheese; sliced cauliflower; shredded carrot; and chives.

For dressing, in a screw-top jar combine salad oil, tarragon vinegar, tarragon, garlic powder, and pepper. Cover and shake well. Pour dressing over pasta mixture. Toss lightly to coat. Cover and chill for 4 to 24 hours.

To serve, line 4 salad plates with lettuce leaves. Divide pasta mixture among lettuce-lined plates. Makes 4 servings.

Time

Preparation	25 min.
Chilling	4 to 24 hrs.

Per Serving

Calories	492
Protein	29 g
Carbohydrate	38 g
Total Fat	25 g
Saturated Fat	8 g
Cholesterol	57 mg
Sodium	840 mg
Potassium	488 mg

Make the Pumpernickel Croutons *and add them to any tossed salad. They will keep for one month in a tightly covered container in the refrigerator.*

PORK AND CABBAGE SALAD

2 cups cubed potatoes (3 medium)

4 cups torn leaf lettuce

2 cups shredded red cabbage

½ pound lean cooked pork, turkey, **or** *beef, cut into bite-size strips (1½ cups)*

1 cup frozen peas, thawed

½ cup Thousand Island Dressing (see recipe, page 205) **or** *Low-Calorie Thousand Island Dressing (see recipe, page 215)*

Pumpernickel Croutons

In a large covered saucepan cook cubed potatoes in a small amount of boiling water for 15 to 20 minutes or till tender. Drain potatoes; place in a medium mixing bowl. Cover and chill for 4 to 24 hours.

❧

To serve, in a large salad bowl combine leaf lettuce and cabbage. Add potatoes; pork, turkey, or beef; and peas. Toss lightly to mix. Pour dressing over salad. Toss lightly to coat. Sprinkle with Pumpernickel Croutons. Makes 4 servings.

Time

Preparation	30 min.
Chilling	4 to 24 hrs.

Per Serving

Calories	545
Protein	27 g
Carbohydrate	55 g
Total Fat	26 g
Saturated Fat	5 g
Cholesterol	72 mg
Sodium	456 mg
Potassium	1,209 mg

PUMPERNICKEL CROUTONS

Cut 2 slices of *pumpernickel bread* into ¾-inch cubes. In a large skillet melt 2 tablespoons *margarine or butter.* Stir in ⅛ teaspoon *onion powder.* Add bread cubes; stir till coated with mixture. Transfer bread cubes to a shallow baking pan. Bake in a 300° oven for 10 minutes. Stir bread cubes. Bake about 5 minutes more or till bread cubes are dry and crisp. Cool.

HAM AND VEGETABLE TOSS

If you're watching calories and fat, replace the dressing with our Oil-Free Dressing (see recipe, page 213) or a purchased reduced-calorie or fat-free salad dressing.

4 cups torn mixed greens

1 cup shredded red cabbage

½ pound lean fully cooked ham, cut into bite-size strips (1½ cups)

1 cup sliced cauliflower flowerets

1 cup frozen peas, thawed

¼ cup sliced radishes

¾ cup Blue Cheese Dressing (see recipe, page 208) **or**

Buttermilk-Herb Dressing (see recipe, page 207)

In a large salad bowl combine mixed greens and red cabbage. Add ham, cauliflower, peas, and radishes. Toss lightly to mix. Pour Blue Cheese Dressing or Buttermilk-Herb Dressing over salad. Toss lightly to coat. Makes 4 servings.

Salads for Lunch

For a light and refreshing brown-bag lunch, pack a cool, crisp salad. Here are a few tips to assure that your salad will be garden-fresh when you are ready to eat it.

● Chill all food thoroughly before packing.

● Pack tossed salads in three separate containers—one for the greens, one for the remaining salad ingredients, and one for the dressing. When you are ready to eat, toss all the ingredients together.

● Pack all salads in insulated containers with frozen ice packs, especially those with meat, poultry, eggs, or a creamy dressing. Be sure to eat your salad lunch within 5 hours of packing it, or keep it refrigerated until you are ready to eat.

Time

Start to finish   30 min.

Per Serving

Calories	265
Protein	23 g
Carbohydrate	12 g
Total Fat	14 g
Saturated Fat	5 g
Cholesterol	48 mg
Sodium	1,034 mg
Potassium	637 mg

To slash the fat content of this delicious pasta salad, choose the ham and yogurt options. Also, use fat-free mayonnaise or salad dressing and low-fat cheese.

SALAMI AND PASTA TOSS

1½ cups corkscrew macaroni (4 ounces)

1½ cups cubed cheddar cheese (6 ounces)

6 ounces salami or lean fully cooked ham, cut into bite-size strips (about 1 cup)

½ cup shredded carrot (1 medium)

½ cup mayonnaise or salad dressing

½ cup dairy sour cream or plain yogurt

2 tablespoons snipped parsley

1 tablespoon snipped fresh basil or 1 teaspoon dried basil, crushed

1 tablespoon Dijon-style mustard

1 cup chopped cucumber (1 small)

1 cup chopped, seeded tomatoes (2 medium)

Time

Preparation	25 min.
Chilling	4 to 24 hrs.

Per Serving

Calories	670
Protein	23 g
Carbohydrate	31 g
Total Fat	52 g
Saturated Fat	20 g
Cholesterol	102 mg
Sodium	1,017 mg
Potassium	453 mg

Cook pasta according to package directions. Drain pasta. Rinse with *cold* water; drain again.

In a large bowl combine pasta, cheese, salami or ham, and carrot.

For dressing, in a small mixing bowl stir together mayonnaise or salad dressing, sour cream or yogurt, parsley, basil, and mustard. Pour dressing over pasta mixture. Toss lightly to coat. Cover and chill for 4 to 24 hours.

Before serving, stir chopped cucumber and tomatoes into the pasta mixture. Makes 4 servings.

DUCK SALAD WITH BEETS AND APPLES

2 whole domestic duckling breasts (about 1½ pounds total) **or** *¾ pound turkey breast tenderloin steaks*

3 medium beets (about ¾ pound) **or** *one 16-ounce can julienne beets, rinsed and drained*

¼ cup walnut oil **or** *salad oil*

3 tablespoons frozen orange juice concentrate, thawed

1 tablespoon white wine vinegar **or** *white vinegar*

⅛ teaspoon pepper

8 cups torn spinach

2 cups coarsely chopped tart green apple (2 medium)

½ cup broken walnuts, toasted

¼ cup crumbled blue cheese **or** *feta cheese*

Concerned about fat? Use turkey instead of the duckling breast and save about 8 grams of fat per serving.

Rinse duckling or turkey; pat dry. For duckling, remove skin and fat; halve each breast. Place duckling (meaty side down) or turkey on the unheated rack of a broiler pan. Broil 4 to 5 inches from the heat for 12 to 15 minutes (broil turkey for 8 to 10 minutes) or till tender and no longer pink, turning once. Cool; cut duckling or turkey into bite-size pieces. Cover and chill for 4 to 24 hours.

❦

In a medium covered saucepan cook fresh beets in boiling water for 40 to 50 minutes or till tender. Drain; cool slightly. Slip skins off beets. Cut beets into julienne strips. Place cooked or canned julienne beets in a medium mixing bowl; set aside.

❦

Meanwhile, for dressing, in a screw-top jar combine walnut or salad oil, orange juice concentrate, vinegar, and pepper. Cover and shake well. Pour *half* of the dressing over the beets. Cover and chill the beets and the remaining dressing for 4 to 24 hours.

❦

To serve, in a large mixing bowl combine duckling or turkey pieces, spinach, and chopped apple. Shake remaining dressing well; pour over duckling mixture. Toss lightly to coat. Divide the duckling mixture among 4 salad plates. Using a slotted spoon, spoon beets over duckling mixture. Sprinkle each serving with walnuts and blue cheese. Makes 4 servings.

Time

Preparation	60 min.
Chilling	4 to 24 hrs.

Per Serving

Calories	452
Protein	21 g
Carbohydrate	26 g
Total Fat	32 g
Saturated Fat	6 g
Cholesterol	52 mg
Sodium	266 mg
Potassium	1,272 mg

DUCK SALAD WITH PEACHES, STRAWBERRIES, AND GLAZED PECANS

Our taste panel rated this salad excellent. The sweet pecans, juicy peaches, and plump strawberries are the perfect complement to the rich, succulent flavor of the duckling.

2 whole domestic duckling breasts (about 1½ pounds total) **or** *¾ pound turkey breast tenderloin steaks*

¼ cup sugar

¾ cup pecan halves

8 cups torn mixed greens

1½ cups sliced, peeled peaches

1½ cups sliced strawberries

3 tablespoons honey

3 tablespoons peach liqueur

⅓ cup salad oil

Nasturtium flowers (optional)

Time

Start to finish   35 min.

Per Serving

Calories	640
Protein	19 g
Carbohydrate	48 g
Total Fat	41 g
Saturated Fat	6 g
Cholesterol	57 mg
Sodium	54 mg
Potassium	726 mg

Rinse duckling or turkey; pat dry. For duckling, remove skin and fat; halve each breast. Place duckling (meaty side down) or turkey on the unheated rack of a broiler pan. Broil 4 to 5 inches from the heat for 12 to 15 minutes (broil turkey for 8 to 10 minutes) or till tender and no longer pink, turning once. Cool; cut duckling or turkey into bite-size pieces. Set aside.

For glazed pecans, place the sugar in a heavy skillet or saucepan. Cook, without stirring, over medium-high heat till the sugar begins to melt, shaking skillet occasionally. Reduce heat to low. Stir with a wooden spoon till the sugar is golden brown and completely melted. Add pecans, stirring to coat. Spread pecans on buttered foil; cool. Break pecans apart.

Meanwhile, in a large salad bowl combine duckling or turkey pieces, torn mixed greens, sliced peaches, and sliced strawberries. Toss lightly to mix. Set aside.

For dressing, in a small mixing bowl combine honey and peach liqueur. Beating with an electric mixer on medium speed, add oil in a thin, steady stream. Continue beating for 2 to 3 minutes more or till mixture is thick. Pour dressing over salad. Sprinkle with pecans. Toss lightly to coat. Divide salad among 4 salad plates. Garnish salads with nasturtium flowers, if desired. Makes 4 servings.

CHICKEN-TORTELLINI SALAD WITH SUN-DRIED TOMATO VINAIGRETTE

This zesty salad also tastes great with cheese ravioli or corkscrew macaroni instead of the tortellini.

2 cups fresh refrigerated cheese-filled tortellini (8 ounces)
1 10-ounce package frozen lima beans, cooked and drained
1½ cups thinly sliced zucchini or yellow summer squash (1 medium)
1¼ cups cooked chicken or turkey cut into bite-size strips (about 6 ounces)
1 small onion, thinly sliced and separated into rings
½ of a 3½-ounce package sliced pepperoni
Sun-Dried Tomato Vinaigrette (see recipe, page 210)
6 cups shredded romaine or spinach

Cook the cheese-filled tortellini according to package directions. Drain tortellini. Rinse with *cold* water; drain again.

❧

In a large mixing bowl combine tortellini, lima beans, zucchini or yellow summer squash, chicken or turkey, onion, and pepperoni. Shake Sun-Dried Tomato Vinaigrette well; pour over salad. Toss lightly to coat. Arrange shredded romaine or spinach on 4 salad plates. Divide tortellini mixture among the salad plates. Makes 4 servings.

Time

Start to finish   35 min.

Per Serving

Calories	512
Protein	33 g
Carbohydrate	54 g
Total Fat	20 g
Saturated Fat	4 g
Cholesterol	76 mg
Sodium	728 mg
Potassium	1,199 mg

Quick-Cooked Chicken

If you need cooked chicken for a recipe but don't have any leftovers, try one of these timesaving options. For 2 cups of cubed, cooked chicken, start with four boned, skinless, medium chicken breast halves (about ¾ pound).

Poaching: In a large skillet place chicken and 1⅓ cups water. Bring to boiling; reduce heat. Cover; simmer for 12 to 14 minutes or till tender. Drain well.

Micro-cooking: Arrange chicken breast halves in an 8x8x2-inch baking dish, tucking under thin portions. Cover with vented clear plastic wrap. Cook on 100-percent power (high) for 8 to 11 minutes or till no longer pink. Rearrange pieces after half of the cooking time. (This timing is for 600- to 700-watt countertop microwave ovens. It is approximate because ovens vary by manufacturer.) Remove from baking dish.

Cut up the cooked chicken. Cover and refrigerate for 2 hours or till thoroughly chilled. To quick-chill the chicken, put it in the freezer for 30 minutes.

STIR-FRY CHICKEN-WALNUT SALAD

Try serving this tasty chicken mixture with rice or couscous instead of the greens.

2 boned skinless chicken breast halves (about ½ pound total)

*8 cups mesclun **or** 6 cups torn romaine and 2 cups torn curly endive, chicory, **or** escarole*

1 large tomato, cut into thin wedges

1 tablespoon salad oil

¾ cup broken walnuts

*1 medium sweet red **or** greeen pepper, cut into ¾-inch pieces (about 1 cup)*

4 green onions, bias-sliced into 1-inch pieces (¾ cup)

½ cup Walnut Vinaigrette (see recipe, page 209)

Rinse chicken; pat dry. Cut the chicken into bite-size strips; set aside.

In a large mixing bowl combine mesclun or romaine and curly endive and tomato wedges. Toss lightly to mix. Divide the greens mixture among 4 salad plates; set aside.

Pour salad oil into a wok or large skillet. (Add more oil as necessary during cooking.) Preheat over medium-high heat. Add walnuts; stir-fry about 1 minute or till lightly toasted. Remove from wok. Add sweet red or green pepper and green onions to the wok; stir-fry for 2 to 3 minutes or till crisp-tender. Remove vegetables from wok.

Add chicken to wok or skillet; stir-fry for 2 to 3 minutes or till no longer pink. Return walnuts and vegetables to wok. Cook and stir about 1 minute or till heated through.

Spoon the hot chicken mixture atop the greens mixture on each salad plate. Serve with Walnut Vinaigrette. Makes 4 servings.

Time

Start to finish   30 min.

Per Serving

Calories	412
Protein	19 g
Carbohydrate	13 g
Total Fat	34 g
Saturated Fat	4 g
Cholesterol	36 mg
Sodium	113 mg
Potassium	680 mg

A *fat-watcher's delight, this healthful salad derives only 18 percent of its calories from fat. Also, it's low in sodium.*

CHICKEN SALAD WITH STRAWBERRY-PEPPERCORN VINAIGRETTE

8 cups mesclun **or** *6 cups torn romaine and 2 cups torn curly endive, chicory,* **or** *escarole*

2½ cups cooked chicken **or** *turkey cut into bite-size strips (about 12 ounces)*

4 ounces enoki mushrooms (about 1½ cups)

1 cup yellow baby pear tomatoes, halved

2 cups sliced, peeled kiwi fruit **or** *sliced carambola (star fruit)*

Strawberry-Peppercorn Vinaigrette

In a large salad bowl combine mesclun or romaine and curly endive, chicken or turkey strips, enoki mushrooms, and tomatoes.

❧

Add kiwi fruit or carambola to salad bowl. Pour Strawberry-Peppercorn Vinaigrette over salad. Toss lightly to coat. Serve immediately. Makes 4 servings.

STRAWBERRY-PEPPERCORN VINAIGRETTE

In a blender container or food processor bowl combine 1 cup cut-up fresh *or* frozen *strawberries* (thaw strawberries, if frozen), 2 tablespoons *red wine vinegar,* and ⅛ teaspoon *cracked black pepper.* Cover and blend or process till smooth. Makes about 1 cup.

Time

Start to finish   25 min.

Per Serving

Calories	239
Protein	30 g
Carbohydrate	19 g
Total Fat	5 g
Saturated Fat	1 g
Cholesterol	74 mg
Sodium	90 mg
Potassium	979 mg

SPICY CHICKEN SALAD WITH HONEY-MUSTARD DRESSING

Crisp oven-fried chicken strips sport a peppery cornmeal coating in this hearty salad.

2 boned skinless chicken breast halves (about ½ pound total)

¼ cup cornmeal

½ teaspoon dried thyme, crushed

¼ teaspoon onion powder

¼ teaspoon garlic salt

¼ teaspoon ground red pepper

2 tablespoons margarine or butter, melted

4 cups torn spinach or romaine

4 cups torn leaf lettuce or iceberg lettuce

2 cups sliced fresh mushrooms

1 cup cubed cheddar, American, or Swiss cheese (4 ounces)

12 cherry tomatoes, halved

½ cup Honey-Mustard Dressing

2 hard-cooked eggs, sliced

Rinse chicken; pat dry. Cut chicken into bite-size strips. In a plastic bag combine cornmeal, thyme, onion powder, garlic salt, red pepper, and ¼ teaspoon *ground black pepper.* Dip chicken strips in melted margarine. Put strips into bag with cornmeal mixture. Close bag; shake to coat chicken. Place chicken strips in a single layer on an ungreased baking sheet. Bake in a 400° oven 8 to 10 minutes or till chicken is tender and no longer pink, turning once.

⚜

Meanwhile, in a large salad bowl combine spinach or romaine, leaf lettuce or iceberg lettuce, mushrooms, cheese, and cherry tomatoes. Add the hot chicken strips. Pour Honey-Mustard Dressing over salad. Toss lightly to coat. Arrange egg slices around edge of salad bowl. Makes 4 servings.

HONEY-MUSTARD DRESSING

In a small mixing bowl or blender container combine ¼ cup *honey,* 3 tablespoons *white wine vinegar or white vinegar,* 2 tablespoons *coarse-grain brown mustard,* and 1 clove *garlic,* minced. Beating with an electric mixer on medium speed or with blender running slowly, add ½ cup *salad oil* in a thin, steady stream. Continue beating or blending about 3 minutes or till thick. Makes about 1 cup.

Time

Start to finish   40 min.

Per Serving

Calories	*505*
Protein	*28 g*
Carbohydrate	*24 g*
Total Fat	*34 g*
Saturated Fat	*10 g*
Cholesterol	*172 mg*
Sodium	*519 mg*
Potassium	*828 mg*

When it's too hot to cook, pull out the fixin's for this easy mix-and-chill salad. The bulgur absorbs the dressing as it chills.

CHICKEN-BULGUR SALAD

¾ cup bulgur

*2 cups chopped cooked **chicken** or **turkey** (about 10 ounces)*

1⅓ cups chopped cucumber (1 medium)

1⅓ cups shredded carrot (3 medium)

1 cup chicken broth

*3 tablespoons **lemon juice** or **lime juice***

*2 tablespoons snipped **fresh basil** or **1 teaspoon dried basil, crushed***

Leaf lettuce leaves

Rinse bulgur in a colander with *cold* water. Drain bulgur. In a large mixing bowl combine bulgur, chicken or turkey, chopped cucumber, and shredded carrot.

For dressing, in a screw-top jar combine chicken broth, lemon juice or lime juice, and basil. Cover and shake well. Pour dressing over chicken mixture. Toss lightly to coat. Cover and chill for 4 to 24 hours or till bulgur has absorbed dressing, stirring occasionally.

To serve, line 4 salad plates with lettuce leaves. Spoon the chicken mixture atop the lettuce. Makes 4 servings.

Time

Preparation	20 min.
Chilling	4 to 24 hrs.

Per Serving

Calories	248
Protein	27 g
Carbohydrate	27 g
Total Fat	4 g
Saturated Fat	2 g
Cholesterol	59 mg
Sodium	267 mg
Potassium	576 mg

Leftover Savvy

Salads are a delicious way to use leftover poultry, meat, and fish. For best flavor and freshness, plan to use your leftover cooked poultry or meat within 4 days. For longer storage, freeze cooked poultry for up to 1 month and cooked meat for up to 3 months. Serve leftover fish no more than 24 hours after cooking it. Do not freeze cooked fish.

CURRIED CHICKEN AND FRUIT SALAD

Serve this twist on a traditional chicken salad with crispy breadsticks.

¾ cup tiny shell macaroni

3 medium oranges

1½ cups halved seedless green or red grapes

1⅓ cups chopped cooked chicken, turkey, or lean beef (about 7 ounces)

1 8-ounce carton lemon low-fat yogurt

¼ cup dairy sour cream

2 tablespoons milk

1 to 2 teaspoons curry powder

Cook pasta according to package directions. Drain pasta. Rinse with *cold* water; drain again.

✻

Meanwhile, peel and section oranges over a bowl to catch the juice. Set the orange sections and juice aside.

✻

In a large salad bowl combine pasta, orange sections and juice, grapes, and cubed chicken, turkey, or beef.

✻

For dressing, in a small mixing bowl stir together lemon yogurt, sour cream, milk, and curry powder. Pour dressing over chicken mixture. Toss lightly to coat. Cover and chill for 4 to 24 hours. Before serving, if necessary, stir in additional milk to moisten. Makes 4 servings.

Time

Preparation	25 min.
Chilling	4 to 24 hrs.

Per Serving

Calories	343
Protein	22 g
Carbohydrate	57 g
Total Fat	4 g
Saturated Fat	1 g
Cholesterol	42 mg
Sodium	82 mg
Potassium	631 mg

For party appetizers, cut this terrific-tasting salad pizza into eight pieces.

CHICKEN SALAD PIZZA

½ of a 17½-ounce package frozen puff pastry (1 sheet)

¼ cup finely snipped sun-dried tomatoes

2 cups torn mixed greens

1½ cups cooked chicken cut into bite-size strips (about 8 ounces)

½ cup sliced pitted ripe olives

⅓ cup soft-style cream cheese with chives and onion

2 teaspoons Dijon-style mustard

3 to 4 tablespoons milk

*1½ cups shredded provolone **or** mozzarella cheese (6 ounces)*

1 medium avocado, seeded, peeled, and sliced

Tomato wedges (optional)

Fresh sage (optional)

Time

Start to finish   45 min.

Per Serving

Calories	719
Protein	36 g
Carbohydrate	36 g
Total Fat	50 g
Saturated Fat	13 g
Cholesterol	95 mg
Sodium	1,009 mg
Potassium	908 mg

Thaw pastry according to package directions. Place pastry on a large baking sheet; generously prick pastry. Bake in a 375° oven for 12 to 15 minutes or till golden.

꙰

Meanwhile, pour enough *boiling water* over the sun-dried tomatoes to cover; let stand for 2 minutes. Drain well. In a large mixing bowl combine the sun-dried tomatoes, greens, chicken, and olives. Toss lightly to mix; set aside.

꙰

For dressing, in a small mixing bowl stir together cream cheese and mustard. Add enough of the milk to make a dressing of drizzling consistency. Drizzle over chicken mixture. Toss lightly to coat.

꙰

Sprinkle *1 cup* of the shredded cheese evenly over the baked pastry. Bake in a 375° oven for 2 to 3 minutes or till cheese melts. Spoon the chicken mixture evenly over the cheese. Arrange the avocado slices on top of the chicken mixture. Sprinkle the remaining ½ cup cheese on top. Bake for 1 to 2 minutes more or till cheese just starts to melt. Cut pizza into squares. Transfer to salad plates. Garnish with tomato wedges and fresh sage, if desired. Serve immediately. Makes 4 servings.

LEMONY CHICKEN SALAD WITH WILD RICE

No chicken or turkey leftovers? Stop by the deli and pick up some cooked poultry for this lemon-flavored salad. Ask to have the chicken or turkey sliced thicker than you would for sandwiches.

Time

Start to finish   55 min.

Per Serving

Calories	430
Protein	33 g
Carbohydrate	33 g
Total Fat	19 g
Saturated Fat	3 g
Cholesterol	74 mg
Sodium	629 mg
Potassium	571 mg

⅓ cup wild rice

1½ cups chicken broth

⅓ cup long grain rice

2½ cups chopped cooked chicken **or** turkey (about 12 ounces)

1 cup halved seedless red **and/or** green grapes

½ cup bias-sliced celery (1 stalk)

½ cup snipped parsley

¼ cup sliced green onion (4 medium)

¼ cup salad oil **or** olive oil

½ teaspoon finely shredded lemon peel

3 tablespoons lemon juice

1 tablespoon Dijon-style mustard

1 tablespoon water

¼ teaspoon salt

¼ teaspoon cracked black pepper

Red-tip leaf lettuce leaves

Lemon peel strips (optional)

Rinse wild rice in a strainer under *cold* running water about 1 minute. In a medium saucepan combine wild rice and chicken broth. Bring to boiling; reduce heat. Cover and simmer for 20 minutes. Stir in the long grain rice. Return to boiling; reduce heat. Cover and simmer about 20 minutes more or till wild rice and long grain rice are tender and liquid is absorbed. Cool rice slightly (about 10 minutes).

⁓

In a large mixing bowl combine the warm rice mixture, chicken or turkey, grapes, celery, parsley, and green onion.

⁓

For dressing, in a screw-top jar combine oil, lemon peel, lemon juice, mustard, water, salt, and cracked pepper. Cover and shake well. Pour dressing over rice mixture. Toss lightly to coat.

⁓

Line 4 salad plates with lettuce leaves. Divide the rice mixture among the lettuce-lined plates. Garnish with lemon peel strips, if desired. Serve immediately. Makes 4 servings.

TWO-ALARM TURKEY AND PASTA SALAD

Here's another serving suggestion: Spoon this Mexican-flavored pasta salad into purchased tortilla bowls lined with shredded lettuce.

1 cup wagon wheel or corkscrew macaroni (4 ounces)

1 15-ounce can black beans, rinsed and drained

1 8¾-ounce can whole kernel corn, drained

1 cup chopped cooked turkey or chicken (about 5 ounces)

1 medium avocado, seeded, peeled, and cut into bite-size chunks (about 1 cup)

½ cup cubed Monterey Jack cheese or Monterey Jack cheese with jalapeño peppers (2 ounces)

¼ cup sliced pitted ripe olives (optional)

1 2-ounce jar diced pimiento, drained

2 tablespoons sliced green onion (2 medium)

3 fresh or canned jalapeño peppers, seeded and chopped (see tip, page 124)

¼ cup salad oil

2 tablespoons white wine vinegar or white vinegar

2 tablespoons lime juice

½ teaspoon chili powder

¼ teaspoon dry mustard

5 or 6 drops bottled hot pepper sauce

Lettuce leaves

Time

Preparation	25 min.
Chilling	4 to 24 hrs.

Per Serving

Calories	570
Protein	27 g
Carbohydrate	53 g
Total Fat	30 g
Saturated Fat	7 g
Cholesterol	40 mg
Sodium	372 mg
Potassium	883 mg

Cook pasta according to package directions. Drain pasta. Rinse with *cold* water; drain again.

❧

In a large mixing bowl combine pasta, black beans, corn, turkey or chicken, avocado, cheese, olives (if desired), pimiento, green onion, and jalapeño peppers.

❧

For dressing, in a screw-top jar combine oil, vinegar, lime juice, chili powder, mustard, and hot pepper sauce. Cover and shake well. Pour dressing over turkey mixture. Toss lightly to coat. Cover and chill for 4 to 24 hours.

❧

To serve, line 4 salad plates with lettuce leaves. Divide turkey mixture among the lettuce-lined plates. Makes 4 servings.

Fire up the grill and get ready to whip up a main-dish version of Waldorf salad—an all-American favorite.

Grilled Chicken Waldorf Salad

⅓ cup mayonnaise **or** *salad dressing*

2 tablespoons honey

1 tablespoon lemon juice

4 boned skinless chicken breast halves (about 1 pound total)

1½ cups chopped apple (1 large)

1 cup seedless red **or** *green grapes, halved*

½ cup thinly sliced celery (1 stalk)

¼ cup chopped walnuts **or** *pecans*

¼ cup raisins

Red **or** *white salad savoy leaves* **or** *savoy cabbage leaves*

For dressing, in a small mixing bowl stir together mayonnaise or salad dressing, honey, and lemon juice. Cover and chill till serving time.

Rinse chicken; pat dry. Grill chicken on an uncovered grill directly over *medium-hot* coals for 15 to 18 minutes or till tender and no longer pink, turning chicken halfway through grilling time. Cool chicken about 20 minutes or till cool enough to handle. Cut chicken into 1-inch pieces.

In a large salad bowl combine chicken, apple, grapes, celery, nuts, and raisins. Pour dressing over salad. Toss lightly to coat. Line 4 salad plates with salad savoy or savoy cabbage leaves. Divide chicken mixture among lettuce-lined plates. Makes 4 servings.

Time

Start to finish 45 *min.**

**Allow extra time to heat the coals.*

Per Serving

Calories	*458*
Protein	*32 g*
Carbohydrate	*29 g*
Total Fat	*24 g*
Saturated Fat	*4 g*
Cholesterol	*74 mg*
Sodium	*266 mg*
Potassium	*439 mg*

Chicken and Pasta Salad with Cilantro Dressing

Rope macaroni sometimes is called gemelli. It looks like two pieces of spaghetti twisted together and cut into short lengths.

1 cup rope macaroni (gemelli) **or** corkscrew macaroni
2½ cups coarsely chopped cooked chicken (about 12 ounces)
1 medium sweet red pepper, seeded **and** cut into thin strips (about 1 cup)
1 medium green pepper, seeded **and** cut into thin strips (about 1 cup)
½ cup sliced pitted ripe olives
Cilantro Dressing
Lettuce leaves

Cook pasta according to package directions. Drain pasta. Rinse with *cold* water; drain again.

In a large mixing bowl combine pasta, chicken, sweet red and green pepper strips, and olives. Shake Cilantro Dressing well; pour over pasta mixture. Toss lightly to coat. Cover and chill for 4 to 24 hours.

To serve, line a salad bowl with lettuce leaves. Transfer pasta mixture to the lettuce-lined salad bowl. Makes 4 servings.

Cilantro Dressing

In a screw-top jar combine ⅓ cup *olive oil or salad oil;* ¼ cup snipped fresh *cilantro;* ¼ cup finely chopped *onion;* ¼ cup *lime juice;* 1 tablespoon *water;* 1 fresh *or* canned *jalapeño pepper,* seeded and finely chopped (see tip, page 124); and 1 clove *garlic,* minced. Cover and shake well. Makes about ¾ cup.

Time

Preparation	25 min.
Chilling	4 to 24 hrs.

Per Serving

Calories	455
Protein	29 g
Carbohydrate	36 g
Total Fat	23 g
Saturated Fat	4 g
Cholesterol	82 mg
Sodium	195 mg
Potassium	590 mg

Team up Oriental vegetables, an Oriental-flavored dressing, and wild rice for a deliciously creative chicken salad.

Sesame Chicken and Rice Salad

⅓ cup wild rice

1 cup water

1 11-ounce can mandarin orange sections, drained

2 cups chopped cooked chicken or turkey (about 10 ounces)

1 cup fresh pea pods or ½ of a 6-ounce package frozen pea pods, thawed

½ cup canned sliced water chestnuts, drained and halved

¼ cup rice wine vinegar or white wine vinegar

3 tablespoons salad oil

1 to 2 teaspoons toasted sesame oil

¼ teaspoon salt

¼ teaspoon ground red pepper

⅛ teaspoon garlic powder

Lettuce leaves

Time

Preparation	1 hr.
Chilling	4 to 24 hrs.

Per Serving

Calories	331
Protein	25 g
Carbohydrate	25 g
Total Fat	15 g
Saturated Fat	2 g
Cholesterol	59 mg
Sodium	202 mg
Potassium	401 mg

Rinse wild rice in a strainer under *cold* running water about 1 minute. In a medium saucepan combine wild rice and water. Bring to boiling; reduce heat. Cover and simmer about 40 minutes or till rice is tender and liquid is absorbed. Cool rice slightly (about 10 minutes).

In a large mixing bowl toss together rice, mandarin orange sections, chicken or turkey, pea pods, and water chestnuts.

For dressing, in a screw-top jar combine vinegar, salad oil, toasted sesame oil, salt, red pepper, and garlic powder. Cover and shake well. Pour dressing over salad. Toss lightly to coat. Cover and chill for 4 to 24 hours.

To serve, line 4 salad plates with lettuce leaves. Divide chicken mixture among the lettuce-lined plates. Make 4 servings.

24-Hour Chicken Fiesta Salad

4 cups torn iceberg lettuce, Boston lettuce, or Bibb lettuce

½ cup shredded Monterey Jack cheese with jalapeño peppers (2 ounces)

1 8-ounce can red kidney beans, rinsed and drained

1½ cups chopped cooked chicken or turkey (about 8 ounces)

2 small tomatoes, cut into thin wedges

1 cup jicama cut into julienne strips (about 4 ounces)

½ cup sliced pitted ripe olives (optional)

Avocado Dressing

¾ cup slighty crushed tortilla chips

Place lettuce in the bottom of a large salad bowl. Layer in the following order: cheese, beans, chicken or turkey, tomatoes, jicama, and, if desired, olives. Spread Avocado Dressing evenly over the top of the salad, sealing to the edge of the bowl. Cover tightly with plastic wrap. Chill for 4 to 24 hours.

❧

Before serving, sprinkle with the crushed tortilla chips. Makes 4 servings.

Avocado Dressing

In a blender container or food processor bowl combine 1 small *avocado*, seeded, peeled, and cut up; ¼ cup *mayonnaise or salad dressing*; 2 tablespoons chopped canned *green chili peppers*; 2 tablespoons *lemon juice*; ½ teaspoon *chili powder*; ¼ teaspoon *salt*; and 1 clove *garlic*, minced. Cover and blend or process till smooth. Makes about ¾ cup.

A layered salad, such as this avocado-topped chicken salad, can simplify your busy life. Make it the night before, and the next day you can come home to dinner waiting in the fridge.

Time

Preparation	30 min.
Chilling	4 to 24 hrs.

Per Serving

Calories	424
Protein	27 g
Carbohydrate	24 g
Total Fat	26 g
Saturated Fat	6 g
Cholesterol	65 mg
Sodium	417 mg
Potassium	847 mg

GRILLED CHICKEN AND VEGETABLE SALAD WITH CHUNKY SALSA

Although any summer squash grills beautifully, we especially liked sunburst and pattypan squash because of their unique shapes.

---

8 yellow sunburst squash **or** *pattypan squash*

4 boned skinless chicken breast halves (about 1 pound total)

4 small zucchini, halved lengthwise

2 large sweet red, yellow, **and/or** *green peppers, cut into 1-inch-wide strips*

2 tablespoons margarine **or** *butter, melted*

White, green, **or** *purple salad savoy leaves, curly endive leaves,* **and/or** *Chinese cabbage leaves*

Chunky Salsa

Precook the squash, covered, in a small amount of boiling water for 3 minutes. Set aside. Rinse chicken; pat dry. Grill chicken on an uncovered grill directly over *medium-hot* coals for 15 to 18 minutes or till tender and no longer pink; turn chicken halfway through grilling time.

❧

Meanwhile, halve the precooked squash. Generously brush squash, zucchini, and sweet pepper strips with melted margarine to prevent vegetables from sticking to grill rack. Lay vegetables on grill rack perpendicular to the bars so they don't fall into coals. Cook vegetables on grill rack with the chicken till tender and slightly charred, turning occasionally. Allow about 18 minutes for squash, 8 to 10 minutes for peppers, and 5 to 6 minutes for zucchini.

❧

Line 4 salad plates with savoy, endive, and/or cabbage leaves. Diagonally cut the chicken breast halves into slices; reassemble breast halves atop greens. Divide vegetables among salad plates. Pour *half* of the Chunky Salsa over salads. Pass the remaining Chunky Salsa. Garnish with white radishes, jalapeño pepper flowers, or habanero peppers, if desired. Serves 4.

CHUNKY SALSA

In a medium mixing bowl stir together 1½ cups finely chopped, peeled *tomatoes;* ½ of a 4-ounce can diced *green chili peppers,* drained; ¼ cup sliced *green onion;* 2 tablespoons chopped *green pepper;* 2 tablespoons snipped fresh *cilantro or parsley;* 2 tablespoons *lemon juice;* 1 clove *garlic;* and ⅛ teaspoon *pepper.* Place about *1 cup* of the tomato mixture and ¼ cup *tomato sauce* in a blender container or food processor bowl. Cover and blend or process just till smooth. Stir into remaining tomato mixture. Cover and chill several hours or overnight, stirring occasionally. Bring to room temperature before serving. Makes about 2 cups.

Time

Preparation	10 min.
Chilling	4 to 24 hrs.
Cooking	25 min.*

Allow extra time to heat coals.

Per Serving

Calories	243
Protein	25 g
Carbohydrate	17 g
Total Fat	9 g
Saturated Fat	2 g
Cholesterol	54 mg
Sodium	380 mg
Potassium	1,199 mg

ARTICHOKE CHICKEN SALAD

When buying artichokes, look for those that are compact and heavy for their size. Also, check for smooth skin and a rounded shape because the roundest artichokes have the largest hearts.

2 medium artichokes (about 10 ounces each)

1 tablespoon lemon juice

8 large romaine leaves

2 cups chopped cooked chicken or turkey (about 10 ounces)

½ cup sliced celery (1 stalk)

¼ cup sliced green onion (4 medium)

¼ cup raisins

½ cup mayonnaise or salad dressing

¼ cup plain yogurt

1 tablespoon snipped chutney

Dash garlic salt

Dash paprika

4 cherry tomatoes, halved

Time

Preparation	30 min.
Cooling	30 min.
Chilling	4 to 24 hrs.

Per Serving

Calories	412
Protein	26 g
Carbohydrate	22 g
Total Fat	26 g
Saturated Fat	4 g
Cholesterol	76 mg
Sodium	362 mg
Potassium	650 mg

Wash artichokes; trim stems and remove loose outer leaves. Cut off 1 inch from each top; snip off the sharp leaf tips. Brush the cut edges with lemon juice. In a large saucepan or Dutch oven bring a large amount of water to boiling. Add artichokes. Return to boiling; reduce heat. Cover and simmer for 20 to 30 minutes or till a leaf pulls out easily. Drain artichokes upside down on paper towels. Spread leaves apart.

When artichokes are cool, pull out all outer leaves; set aside. Pull out and discard center leaves (cone). Scrape out chokes with a spoon; discard the chokes and reserve the hearts. Cut the hearts into thin strips (you should have about ⅓ cup). Wrap the reserved artichoke leaves and heart strips in plastic wrap and chill.

Finely shred *two* of the romaine leaves. In a large salad bowl combine shredded romaine, chicken or turkey, sliced celery, sliced green onion, and raisins.

For dressing, in a small mixing bowl stir together mayonnaise or salad dressing, yogurt, chutney, garlic salt, and paprika. Pour dressing over chicken mixture. Toss lightly to coat. Cover and chill for 4 to 24 hours.

To serve, line a serving platter with remaining romaine leaves. Spoon chicken mixture into center of platter. Arrange reserved artichoke heart strips atop chicken mixture. Arrange reserved artichoke leaves and halved cherry tomatoes around edge of platter. Serves 4.

CHICKEN SALAD BUNDLES WITH SAVOY AND RADICCHIO

1 head savoy cabbage **or** Chinese cabbage

1 head radicchio

2 cups chopped cooked chicken (about 10 ounces)

1 cup finely chopped fresh pineapple **or** one 8¼-ounce can crushed pineapple, drained

2 tablespoons thinly sliced green onion (2 medium)

¼ cup raisins

¼ cup unsalted cocktail peanuts, chopped (optional)

¾ cup mayonnaise **or** salad dressing

¼ cup milk

¼ cup peanut butter

1 teaspoon curry powder

½ teaspoon paprika

¼ teaspoon lemon juice **or** lime juice

1 to 2 tablespoons milk

Instead of radicchio, you can use red cabbage. Remove 16 of the outer leaves and then shred about half of the remaining cabbage.

Remove 8 of the large outer leaves from the cabbage. Immerse the leaves, 4 at a time, into *boiling* water about 3 minutes or till limp. Drain well. Cover and chill in the refrigerator. Remove 16 of the large leaves from the radicchio. *Do not cook.* Cover leaves and chill.

⬩⚘⬩

Meanwhile, coarsely shred the remaining cabbage and radicchio. Measure *1½ cups* of the shredded mixture. Set the remaining shredded mixture aside. In a large bowl combine the 1½ cups shredded mixture, chicken, pineapple, green onion, raisins, and, if desired, peanuts.

⬩⚘⬩

For dressing, combine mayonnaise, the ¼ cup milk, peanut butter, curry powder, paprika, and lemon juice. Pour ½ *cup* dressing over chicken mixture. Stir lightly to coat. Stir the 1 to 2 tablespoons milk into the remaining dressing till it reaches drizzling consistency. Set aside.

⬩⚘⬩

For each cabbage roll, place about ½ *cup* of the chicken mixture at 1 end of *each* cabbage leaf. Fold in the sides of the leaf. Roll the leaf around the chicken mixture.

⬩⚘⬩

Line 4 salad plates with the remaining shredded mixture, the 16 radicchio leaves, and, if desired, salad savoy leaves. Top each plate with 2 cabbage rolls. Pass the remaining dressing. Makes 4 servings.

Time

Start to finish	1 hr.

Per Serving

Calories	623
Protein	31 g
Carbohydrate	30 g
Total Fat	45 g
Saturated Fat	8 g
Cholesterol	85 mg
Sodium	420 mg
Potassium	866 mg

ORIENTAL CHICKEN SALAD

Serve this gingery chicken salad with crisp crackers. And, for dessert, dish up some refreshing lemon sherbet.

4 boned skinless chicken breast halves (about 1 pound total)

3 tablespoons soy sauce

2 teaspoons grated gingerroot

5 cups torn mixed greens

3 cups assorted vegetables (fresh bean sprouts; fresh pea pods, strings removed and halved crosswise; and/or julienne strips of cucumber)

1 cup coarsely chopped red cabbage

¼ cup sliced green onion (4 medium)

1 3-ounce package Oriental noodles (with or without flavor packet)

Oriental Salad Dressing

Purple salad savoy leaves (optional)

2 teaspoons sesame seed, toasted

Time

Start to finish   35 min.

Per Serving

Calories	232
Protein	25 g
Carbohydrate	19 g
Total Fat	7 g
Saturated Fat	1 g
Cholesterol	54 mg
Sodium	653 mg
Potassium	618 mg

Rinse chicken; pat dry. Place chicken breasts on the greased unheated rack of a broiler pan. Stir together the soy sauce and gingerroot; brush some onto chicken. Broil 4 inches from heat for 12 to 15 minutes, turning once and brushing with the remaining soy mixture. Remove from heat; cool slightly. Cut chicken into bite-size strips; set aside.

In a large mixing bowl toss together the mixed greens, assorted vegetables, red cabbage, and green onion. Break dry Oriental noodles into small pieces; add to salad. (Reserve flavor packet for another use.)

Shake Oriental Salad Dressing well; pour about ½ cup of the dressing over salad. Toss lightly to coat. Line 4 salad plates with salad savoy leaves, if desired. Divide salad among plates. Top each salad with one-fourth of the chicken strips; pour remaining dressing over chicken. Sprinkle with sesame seed. Serve immediately. Makes 4 servings.

ORIENTAL SALAD DRESSING

In a screw-top jar combine ⅓ cup unsweetened pineapple juice, ¼ cup rice vinegar or white vinegar, 1 tablespoon soy sauce, 2 teaspoons sugar, 1½ teaspoons toasted sesame oil, and ¼ teaspoon pepper. Cover and shake well. Makes about ⅔ cup.

SALMON AND PASTA SALAD

1½ cups medium shell macaroni (4 ounces)

1 cup frozen cut green beans

⅓ cup sliced pitted ripe olives

½ cup mayonnaise or salad dressing

2 tablespoons white wine Worcestershire sauce

1 tablespoon snipped fresh basil or 1 teaspoon dried basil, crushed

1 tablespoon snipped fresh oregano or 1 teaspoon dried oregano, crushed

⅛ teaspoon garlic powder

1 15½-ounce can salmon, drained, flaked, and skin and bones removed

Milk

¼ cup sliced radishes

Leaf lettuce leaves

In a large saucepan cook pasta in boiling water for 8 minutes. Add frozen green beans; return to boiling. Cook about 5 minutes more or till pasta and beans are tender. Drain pasta and beans. Rinse with *cold* water; drain again.

❧

In a large mixing bowl combine pasta, green beans, and olives.

❧

For dressing, in a small mixing bowl stir together mayonnaise or salad dressing, white wine Worcestershire sauce, basil, oregano, and garlic powder. Pour dressing over the pasta mixture. Add salmon. Toss lightly to mix. Cover and chill for 4 to 24 hours.

❧

Before serving, if necessary, stir a little milk into the salad to moisten. Line 4 salad plates with lettuce leaves. Divide salad among plates. Garnish each plate with radishes. Makes 4 servings.

To reduce the fat in this creamy salad, switch the salmon to two 6½-ounce cans water-pack tuna, reduce the olives to 2 tablespoons, and use nonfat mayonnaise or salad dressing.

Time

Preparation	*30 min.*
Chilling	*4 to 24 hrs.*

Per Serving

Calories	*487*
Protein	*25 g*
Carbohydrate	*28 g*
Total Fat	*31 g*
Saturated Fat	*5 g*
Cholesterol	*60 mg*
Sodium	*879 mg*
Potassium	*524 mg*

When buying fresh tuna, look for dark red flesh with a slightly oily sheen.

WARM TUNA AND GINGER SALAD

¾ pound fresh or frozen tuna or halibut steaks, cut 1 inch thick

1 teaspoon lemon juice

1 teaspoon soy sauce

3 cups coarsely chopped Chinese cabbage

2 cups coarsely chopped bok choy

1 11-ounce can mandarin orange sections, drained

1 cup fresh bean sprouts

1 medium onion, halved and sliced

2 teaspoons grated gingerroot

1 clove garlic, minced

1 tablespoon salad oil

2 tablespoons lemon juice

2 tablespoons dry sherry

2 tablespoons water

1 teaspoon toasted sesame oil

2 teaspoons sesame seed, toasted

Time

Start to finish   30 min.

Per Serving

Calories	250
Protein	22 g
Carbohydrate	18 g
Total Fat	10 g
Saturated Fat	2 g
Cholesterol	32 mg
Sodium	131 mg
Potassium	600 mg

Thaw fish, if frozen. Combine the 1 teaspoon lemon juice and the soy sauce; brush on both sides of the tuna or halibut steaks. Place the steaks on the greased unheated rack of a broiler pan. Broil 4 inches from the heat for 12 to 16 minutes or till fish just begins to flake easily with a fork, turning once. Cut the fish into bite-size pieces.

⚜

Meanwhile, in a large salad bowl combine the Chinese cabbage, bok choy, mandarin orange sections, and bean sprouts. Set aside.

⚜

In a medium skillet cook onion, gingerroot, and garlic in hot oil till onion is tender but not brown, stirring constantly. Remove from heat. Stir the 2 tablespoons lemon juice, dry sherry, water, and sesame oil into the onion mixture in the skillet. Heat through. Add fish pieces and onion mixture to cabbage mixture. Toss lightly to mix. Sprinkle with sesame seed. Serve warm. Makes 4 servings.

SORREL AND SOLE SALAD

1 pound fresh **or** *frozen skinless sole* **or** *flounder fillets*

½ cup dry white wine, chicken broth, **or** *water*

½ pound asparagus spears, bias-cut into 2-inch pieces

3 tablespoons salad oil

3 tablespoons tarragon vinegar

1 tablespoon snipped parsley

1 tablespoon sliced green onion (1 medium)

1 tablespoon capers, drained

¼ teaspoon salt

⅛ teaspoon pepper

4 cups torn sorrel **or** *leaf lettuce*

Thaw fish, if frozen. Measure thickness of fish. Pour wine, chicken broth, or water into a large skillet. Bring to boiling. Add fish. Return to boiling; reduce heat. Cover and simmer till fish just begins to flake easily with a fork (allow 4 to 6 minutes for each ½-inch thickness of fish). Using a slotted spoon, remove fish from skillet. Cover and refrigerate fish for 2 hours or till thoroughly chilled. Discard cooking liquid.

In a covered saucepan cook asparagus in a small amount of boiling water for 5 to 8 minutes or till crisp-tender. Drain the asparagus. Cover and refrigerate asparagus for 2 hours or till thoroughly chilled.

For dressing, in a screw-top jar combine oil, vinegar, parsley, green onion, capers, salt, and pepper. Cover and shake well.

Line 4 salad plates with sorrel or leaf lettuce. Break the chilled fish into bite-size chunks. Arrange fish chunks and asparagus on the sorrel. Shake dressing well; pour over salads. Makes 4 servings.

Tender and lemony in flavor, sorrel is the perfect green for mild and sweet-flavored fish such as sole and flounder.

Time

Preparation	15 min.
Chilling	2 hrs.
Assembling	15 min.

Per Serving

Calories	302
Protein	22 g
Carbohydrate	9 g
Total Fat	19 g
Saturated Fat	1 g
Cholesterol	23 mg
Sodium	240 mg
Potassium	737 mg

Salmon is one fish that contains a substance called omega-3 fatty acid. Some experts believe this fatty acid may help lower blood cholesterol levels in humans. It's also found in lake and rainbow trout, tuna, and swordfish.

Time

Preparation	35 min.
Chilling	4 to 24 hrs.

Per Serving

Calories	614
Protein	30 g
Carbohydrate	34 g
Total Fat	40 g
Saturated Fat	7 g
Cholesterol	176 mg
Sodium	941 mg
Potassium	1,168 mg

DILLED SALMON-POTATO SALAD

3 medium red potatoes (about 1 pound)

⅔ cup mayonnaise or salad dressing

⅓ cup plain yogurt

4 teaspoons snipped fresh dill or 1 teaspoon dried dillweed

1 tablespoon milk

½ teaspoon lemon-pepper seasoning

¼ teaspoon garlic powder

1 cup chopped cucumber (1 small)

¼ cup sliced green onion (4 medium)

1½ cups flaked, cooked salmon (½ pound) or one 15½-ounce can salmon, drained, flaked, and skin and bones removed

2 hard-cooked eggs, chopped

Red-tip leaf lettuce leaves

4 cups shredded red-tip leaf lettuce

Sieved hard-cooked egg yolk (optional)

Cucumber spears (optional)

Fresh dill (optional)

Cut unpeeled potatoes into ¾-inch cubes. In a covered saucepan cook potatoes in boiling water for 12 to 15 minutes or till just tender. Drain well. Cool slightly.

❦

Meanwhile, for dressing, in a small mixing bowl stir together mayonnaise or salad dressing, yogurt, dill, milk, lemon-pepper seasoning, and garlic powder.

❦

In a large mixing bowl combine the dressing, chopped cucumber, and sliced green onion. Add cooked potatoes, salmon, and the 2 hard-cooked eggs. Toss lightly to mix. Cover and chill for 4 to 24 hours.

❦

To serve, line 4 salad plates with lettuce leaves. Top each plate with *1 cup* of the shredded lettuce. Divide the salmon mixture among the lettuce-lined plates. Garnish with sieved hard-cooked egg yolk, cucumber spears and fresh dill, if desired. Makes 4 servings.

Choosing a firm-textured fish for this salad ensures that the fish will stay in attractive chunks. Besides cod, our Test Kitchen home economists recommend orange roughy, grouper, scrod, and red snapper.

Time

Preparation	15 min.
Chilling	2 hrs.
Assembling	15 min.

Per Serving

Calories	293
Protein	22 g
Carbohydrate	17 g
Total Fat	15 g
Saturated Fat	2 g
Cholesterol	47 mg
Sodium	371 mg
Potassium	788 mg

TOSSED FISH SALAD

1 pound fresh or frozen skinless cod or other firm-textured fish fillets

¼ cup dry white wine or water

¼ cup water

¼ teaspoon salt

3 oranges

Orange juice

¼ cup salad oil

1½ teaspoons snipped fresh thyme or ½ teaspoon dried thyme, crushed

¼ teaspoon salt

¼ teaspoon pepper or lemon-pepper seasoning

3 cups torn red-tip leaf lettuce or leaf lettuce

3 cups torn spinach

1 small red onion, sliced and separated into rings

Thaw fish, if frozen. Cut fish into 1-inch pieces. In a large skillet combine wine, water, and ¼ teaspoon salt. Bring to boiling. Add fish. Return to boiling; reduce heat. Cover and simmer for 3 to 6 minutes or till fish just begins to flake easily with a fork. Using a slotted spoon, carefully remove fish pieces from skillet. Cover and refrigerate fish for 2 hours or till thoroughly chilled. Discard cooking liquid.

Finely shred enough peel from 1 of the oranges to equal ½ teaspoon. Set orange peel aside. Working over a mixing bowl to catch the juices, peel and section the oranges. Set orange sections aside. Transfer the juice to a measuring cup. Add enough additional orange juice to equal ¼ cup.

For dressing, in a screw-top jar combine the orange peel, the ¼ cup orange juice, salad oil, thyme, ¼ teaspoon salt, and pepper or lemon-pepper seasoning. Cover and shake well.

In a large salad bowl combine lettuce, spinach, and onion rings. Toss lightly to mix. Add fish pieces and orange sections. Shake dressing well; pour over salad. Toss lightly to coat. Serves 4.

TARRAGON SALMON SALAD

1 pound fresh or *frozen skinless salmon fillets*

Salad oil

1 8-ounce carton plain yogurt

⅔ cup snipped parsley

1 tablespoon snipped fresh tarragon or *1 teaspoon dried tarragon, crushed*

1 clove garlic, minced

Spinach leaves or *romaine leaves*

2 medium tomatoes, cut into wedges

1⅓ cups thinly sliced cucumber (1 small)

1 small green pepper, cut into bite-size strips

The fresh-tasting yogurt dressing makes an equally good sauce to serve with grilled or broiled salmon steaks or fillets.

Thaw fish, if frozen. Cut into 4 serving-size portions. Measure thickness of fish. Place fish on the greased unheated rack of a broiler pan. Brush fish with oil. Broil 4 inches from the heat till fish just begins to flake easily with a fork. (Allow 4 to 6 minutes for each ½-inch thickness of fish. If fish is 1 inch or more thick, turn it over and brush with additional oil halfway through cooking.)

Meanwhile, for dressing, in a mixing bowl stir together yogurt, parsley, tarragon, and garlic.

Line 4 salad plates with spinach or romaine leaves. Place a piece of fish in the center of each plate. Arrange tomato wedges, cucumber slices, and green pepper strips around the fish. Pour some of the dressing over the fish and vegetables; pass remaining dressing. Makes 4 servings.

Time

Start to finish   25 min.

Per Serving

Calories	*233*
Protein	*22 g*
Carbohydrate	*11 g*
Total Fat	*11 g*
Saturated Fat	*3 g*
Cholesterol	*60 mg*
Sodium	*102 mg*
Potassium	*867 mg*

Snipping Fresh Herbs

Since many salads call for snipped fresh herbs, here's the easiest way to snip them. Place several sprigs in a deep container such as a 1-cup measuring cup. With kitchen shears, snip the herb in the container until the herb is in fine pieces. If you would rather use dried herbs instead of fresh, use only one-third of the amount.

The outer leaves of a head of iceberg lettuce are the best for making bundles because they are larger and more flexible than the inner leaves.

TUNA-ALMOND SALAD BUNDLES

*⅔ cup mayonnaise **or** salad dressing*

2 tablespoons snipped parsley

½ teaspoon finely shredded lemon peel

1 9¼-ounce can tuna (water pack), drained and broken into chunks

½ cup sliced celery (1 stalk)

2 tablespoons sliced green onion (2 medium)

1 cup chopped apple (1 medium)

¼ cup slivered almonds, toasted

*8 leaf lettuce leaves **or** iceberg lettuce leaves*

For dressing, in a small mixing bowl stir together mayonnaise or salad dressing, snipped parsley, and lemon peel.

In a large mixing bowl combine tuna, celery, and green onion. Gently stir the dressing into the tuna mixture. Cover and chill for 1 to 24 hours.

For bundles, stir apple and almonds into tuna mixture. Cut the rib from each leaf lettuce leaf or the heavy base from each iceberg lettuce leaf. Place about *⅓ cup* of the tuna mixture in the center of *each* lettuce leaf. Fold in the sides of the leaf. Roll the leaf around the tuna mixture. To serve, place *two* bundles on *each* salad plate. Makes 4 servings.

Time

Preparation	15 min.
Chilling	1 to 24 hrs.
Assembling	15 min.

Per Serving

Calories	421
Protein	22 g
Carbohydrate	9 g
Total Fat	34 g
Saturated Fat	5 g
Cholesterol	58 mg
Sodium	454 mg
Potassium	420 mg

ORANGE ROUGHY AND POTATO TOSS

1 pound fresh **or** *frozen skinless orange roughy, cod,* **or** *other firm-textured fish fillets*

1 pound whole tiny new potatoes, quartered (about 12)

½ cup water

¼ teaspoon salt

1 cup frozen peas, thawed

⅔ cup Thousand Island Dressing (see recipe, page 205)

Lettuce leaves

Thaw fish, if frozen. Measure thickness of fish. In a covered saucepan cook potatoes in boiling water for 12 to 15 minutes or till tender. Drain well. Cover and refrigerate for 2 hours or till thoroughly chilled.

❧

Meanwhile, in a large skillet combine water and salt. Bring to boiling. Add fish. Return to boiling; reduce heat. Cover and simmer till fish just begins to flake easily with a fork (allow 4 to 6 minutes for each ½-inch thickness of fish). Using a slotted spoon, carefully remove fish from the skillet. Cover and refrigerate for 2 hours or till thoroughly chilled. Discard cooking liquid.

❧

To serve, in a large mixing bowl combine potatoes and peas. Add Thousand Island Dressing. Toss lightly to coat. Break the fish into bite-size pieces; add fish to potato mixture. Toss gently to mix. Line a large salad bowl with lettuce leaves. Transfer potato mixture to the lettuce-lined bowl. Makes 4 servings.

New potatoes are most readily available in late spring and through the summer. If you would like to make this salad in the fall or winter, use round red or round white potatoes cut into bite-size chunks.

Time

Preparation	*30 min.*
Chilling	*2 hrs.*

Per Serving

Calories	*486*
Protein	*23 g*
Carbohydrate	*35 g*
Total Fat	*29 g*
Saturated Fat	*3 g*
Cholesterol	*61 mg*
Sodium	*526 mg*
Potassium	*611 mg*

We've invented a new version of taco salad that uses poached fish instead of beef and a creamy dressing instead of salsa.

MEXICAN FISH SALAD

1 pound fresh or frozen skinless orange roughy or other firm-textured fish fillets

½ cup water

¼ teaspoon salt

¼ cup mayonnaise or salad dressing

¼ cup dairy sour cream

1 jalapeño pepper, seeded and chopped (see tip, page 124)

1 tablespoon milk

1 tablespoon snipped fresh oregano or ½ teaspoon dried oregano, crushed

¼ teaspoon garlic powder

Several dashes bottled hot pepper sauce

4 cups shredded lettuce

1 large avocado, seeded, peeled, and cut into bite-size pieces

1 cup shredded cheddar or Monterey Jack cheese (4 ounces)

1 cup chopped, seeded tomato (1 large)

½ cup shredded carrot (1 medium)

⅓ cup sliced pitted ripe olives (optional)

4 purchased tortilla cups or 4 cups tortilla chips

Time

Preparation	15 min.
Chilling	2 hrs.
Assembling	20 min.

Per Serving

Calories	648
Protein	29 g
Carbohydrate	28 g
Total Fat	49 g
Saturated Fat	12 g
Cholesterol	68 mg
Sodium	660 mg
Potassium	690 mg

Thaw fish, if frozen. Cut fish into 1-inch pieces. In a large skillet combine water and salt. Bring to boiling. Add fish. Return to boiling; reduce heat. Cover and simmer for 3 to 6 minutes or till fish just begins to flake easily with a fork. Using a slotted spoon, carefully remove fish from the skillet. Cover and refrigerate fish for 2 hours or till thoroughly chilled. Discard cooking liquid.

For dressing, in a small mixing bowl stir together mayonnaise or salad dressing, sour cream, jalapeño pepper, milk, oregano, garlic powder, and bottled hot pepper sauce.

In a large mixing bowl combine shredded lettuce, avocado, cheese, tomato, carrot, and, if desired, olives. Toss lightly to mix. Divide the lettuce mixture among tortilla cups or 4 salad plates lined with tortilla chips. Top each serving with some fish and a dollop of dressing. Makes 4 servings.

CURRIED TUNA AND EGG SALAD

Spread this tuna mixture on slices of bread for great-tasting sandwiches.

½ cup mayonnaise **or** salad dressing

½ cup chopped celery (1 stalk)

¼ cup sliced green onion (4 medium)

3 tablespoons snipped chutney

2 teaspoons curry powder

1 6½-ounce can chunk white tuna, drained and broken into chunks

4 hard-cooked eggs, chopped

4 large tomatoes

Lettuce leaves

¼ cup raisins

In a large mixing bowl stir together mayonnaise or salad dressing, celery, green onion, chutney, and curry powder. Gently fold in the tuna and the hard-cooked eggs. Cover and chill for 1 to 24 hours.

✤

To serve, cut out ½ inch of the core from each tomato. Invert tomatoes. Cutting from the top to, *but not through,* the stem end, cut each tomato into 6 wedges. Spread wedges slightly apart.

✤

Line 4 salad plates with lettuce leaves. Place tomatoes on the lettuce-lined plates. Spoon *one-fourth* of the tuna mixture into the center of *each* tomato. Sprinkle with raisins. Serves 4.

Time

Preparation	35 min.
Chilling	1 to 24 hrs.
Assembling	10 min.

Per Serving

Calories	434
Protein	21 g
Carbohydrate	27 g
Total Fat	28 g
Saturated Fat	5 g
Cholesterol	252 mg
Sodium	520 mg
Potassium	633 mg

CURRIED SEAFOOD AND PASTA SALAD

Why do we call for water-pack instead of oil-pack tuna in our recipes? Because for every 3 ounces of tuna, you'll save yourself 17 grams of fat.

1½ cups corkscrew macaroni (4 ounces)

1 6½-ounce can tuna (water pack), drained and broken into chunks

1 6-ounce package frozen, peeled, cooked shrimp, thawed

¾ cup thinly sliced celery (1½ stalks)

¼ cup snipped parsley

*½ cup mayonnaise **or** salad dressing*

2 tablespoons lemon juice

1 tablespoon milk

3 to 4 teaspoons curry powder

¼ teaspoon salt

1 large clove garlic, minced

Time

Preparation	25 min.
Chilling	4 to 24 hrs.

Per Serving

Calories	478
Protein	27 g
Carbohydrate	40 g
Total Fat	24 g
Saturated Fat	4 g
Cholesterol	120 mg
Sodium	542 mg
Potassium	513 mg

Cook pasta according to package directions. Drain pasta. Rinse with *cold* water; drain again.

❧

In a large mixing bowl combine pasta, tuna, shrimp, celery, and parsley.

❧

For dressing, in a small mixing bowl stir together mayonnaise or salad dressing, lemon juice, milk, curry powder, salt, and garlic. Pour dressing over pasta mixture. Toss lightly to coat. Cover and chill for 4 to 24 hours.

❧

Before serving, if necessary, stir in additional milk to moisten. Makes 4 servings.

CRAB SALAD WITH MELONS

An herb-flavored mayonnaise dressing accents the slightly sweet crabmeat in this light and fresh seafood salad.

½ cup mayonnaise **or** salad dressing

2 tablespoons snipped parsley

1 tablespoon chili sauce

1½ teaspoons snipped fresh tarragon **or** ½ teaspoon dried tarragon, crushed

1½ teaspoons snipped fresh basil **or** ½ teaspoon dried basil, crushed

⅛ teaspoon ground red pepper

1 clove garlic, halved

½ cup finely chopped sweet red **or** green pepper (1 small)

½ cup chopped celery (1 stalk)

12 ounces coarsely flaked, cooked crabmeat (2¼ cups) **or** three 4-ounce packages frozen, crab-flavored, salad-style fish

Red-tip leaf lettuce leaves **or** romaine leaves

½ of a small cantaloupe, seeded, peeled, and thinly sliced

½ of a small honeydew melon, seeded, peeled, and thinly sliced

For dressing, in a blender container or food processor bowl combine mayonnaise or salad dressing, parsley, chili sauce, tarragon, basil, ground red pepper, and garlic. Cover and blend or process till smooth. Set dressing aside.

❧

In a medium mixing bowl combine sweet red or green pepper, celery, and ¼ cup of the dressing. Gently fold in the crabmeat.

❧

Line 4 salad plates with lettuce leaves. Arrange cantaloupe and honeydew melon slices atop lettuce leaves. Spoon salad over melon slices. Dollop each salad with additional dressing. Makes 4 servings.

Time

Start to finish   25 min.

Per Serving

Calories	360
Protein	19 g
Carbohydrate	20 g
Total Fat	23 g
Saturated Fat	4 g
Cholesterol	92 mg
Sodium	530 mg
Potassium	973 mg

The contrasting colors and varied textures of the fruit and seafood make this a perfect spring luncheon salad.

SHRIMP SALAD WITH BERRY VINAIGRETTE

¾ pound asparagus spears **or** *one 10-ounce package frozen asparagus spears*

1 8-ounce package frozen baby corn

12 ounces fresh **or** *frozen peeled and deveined shrimp*

12 Belgian endive leaves

12 Boston **or** *Bibb lettuce leaves*

12 sorrel **or** *spinach leaves*

2½ to 3 cups fresh **or** *frozen red raspberries* **and/or** *sliced strawberries, thawed*

Berry Vinaigrette

Fresh cilantro (optional)

Time

Start to finish   25 min.

Per Serving

Calories	*345*
Protein	*20 g*
Carbohydrate	*28 g*
Total Fat	*19 g*
Saturated Fat	*2 g*
Cholesterol	*125 mg*
Sodium	*161 mg*
Potassium	*778 mg*

Snap off and discard woody bases from fresh asparagus. If desired, scrape off scales. Cook asparagus, covered, in a small amount of boiling water for 4 to 8 minutes or till tender. (*Or,* cook frozen asparagus according to package directions.) Cook frozen baby corn according to package directions.

Meanwhile, bring 4 cups *water* and 1 teaspoon *salt* to boiling. Add shrimp. Simmer, uncovered, for 1 to 3 minutes or till shrimp turn pink, stirring occasionally. Drain shrimp and rinse under cold running water.

Arrange Belgian endive leaves, Boston or Bibb leaves, sorrel or spinach leaves, and asparagus on 4 salad plates. Divide the baby corn among the salad plates, placing it atop the Belgian endive. Divide the shrimp among the salad plates, placing it atop the Boston or Bibb lettuce. Divide the berries among the salad plates, placing them atop the sorrel or spinach leaves. Pour Berry Vinaigrette over the salads. Garnish with cilantro, if desired. Makes 4 servings.

BERRY VINAIGRETTE

In a screw-top jar mix ¼ cup *walnut oil or salad oil,* ¼ cup *raspberry or strawberry vinegar,* 1 tablespoon snipped fresh *cilantro or parsley,* and 2 teaspoons *honey.* Cover; shake well.

Fresh sorrel gives the rich dressing a lemony zip.

Shrimp Salad With Creamy Sorrel Dressing

12 ounces fresh **or** *frozen cooked shrimp*

1 medium cucumber, halved lengthwise and thinly sliced (1¾ cup)

1 small red onion, sliced and separated into rings

¼ cup thinly sliced celery

⅓ cup whipping cream

½ teaspoon finely shredded lemon peel

⅛ teaspoon salt

½ cup finely snipped sorrel

¼ cup mayonnaise **or** *salad dressing*

Sorrel leaves

Time

Preparation	15 min.
Chilling	2 to 3 hrs.
Assembling	10 min.

Per Serving

Calories	278
Protein	21 g
Carbohydrate	6 g
Total Fat	20 g
Saturated Fat	6 g
Cholesterol	201 mg
Sodium	353 mg
Potassium	533 mg

Thaw shrimp, if frozen. In a medium mixing bowl combine the shrimp, cucumber, onion, and celery. Cover and chill for 2 to 3 hours.

❧

For dressing, in a small mixing bowl beat the whipping cream, lemon peel, and salt with an electric mixer on low speed till soft peaks form. Fold in the ½ cup snipped sorrel and the mayonnaise or salad dressing.

❧

Line 4 salad plates with sorrel leaves. Top with shrimp mixture. Dollop shrimp mixture with dressing. Makes 4 servings.

SUSHI-STYLE SHRIMP SALAD

2 medium carrots, cut into julienne strips (1 cup)

¼ teaspoon chili oil

1 cup fresh pea pods **or** *½ of a 6-ounce package frozen pea pods, thawed*

1 teaspoon toasted sesame oil

24 fresh **or** *frozen medium shrimp in shells (about ¾ pound)*

Vinegared Rice

Place carrots in a small bowl. Stir chili oil into carrots; set aside. Cook pea pods, covered, in a small amount of boiling water for 2 to 4 minutes or till crisp-tender. Drain and place in another small bowl. Stir sesame oil into pea pods; set aside.

❧

Thaw shrimp, if frozen. Peel and devein shrimp, leaving tails intact. Bring 4 cups *water* and 1 teaspoon *salt* to boiling. Add shrimp. Simmer, uncovered, for 1 to 3 minutes or till shrimp turn pink, stirring occasionally. Drain shrimp and rinse under cold running water.

❧

To serve, mound about *½ cup* Vinegared Rice into the center of 4 salad plates. Divide carrots among salad plates, placing them to the left of the rice. Divide pea pods among salad plates, placing them to the right of the rice. Place *six* shrimp on *each* salad plate, three at the top of the rice and three at the bottom. Makes 4 servings.

VINEGARED RICE

Wash ½ cup *short or long grain rice* under cold running water, rubbing grains together with fingers, till water runs clear. Drain. In a medium saucepan combine rice, 1 cup *cold water,* and ¼ teaspoon *salt.* Bring to boiling; reduce heat to low and cover with a tight-fitting lid. Simmer for 15 minutes. Remove from heat. Stir 3 tablespoon snipped *chives or* sliced *green onion tops,* 4 teaspoons *rice vinegar or white vinegar,* 1 tablespoon *sugar,* and 1 tablespoon *mirin or dry sherry* into the rice. Cover rice mixture and cool to room temperature. Makes about 2 cups.

Sushi is a Japanese delicacy featuring vinegared cooked rice that is wrapped in fish or seaweed. Our Oriental salad captures the essence of sushi with less effort—the rice simply is surrounded by shrimp and seasoned vegetables.

Time

Start to finish   45 min.

Per Serving

Calories	*194*
Protein	*14 g*
Carbohydrate	*28 g*
Total Fat	*2 g*
Saturated Fat	*0 g*
Cholesterol	*97 mg*
Sodium	*260 mg*
Potassium	*314 mg*

SHRIMP LOUIS SLAW

Reduce the cholesterol in this take-off on the classic Crab Louis salad by leaving out the hard-cooked eggs.

12 ounces fresh or frozen peeled and deveined shrimp

½ cup mayonnaise or salad dressing

¼ cup sliced green onion (4 medium)

2 tablespoons chili sauce

½ teaspoon finely shredded lemon peel

1 teaspoon lemon juice

1 teaspoon prepared horseradish

4 small tomatoes, thinly sliced

4 cups shredded Chinese cabbage and/or cabbage and/or romaine

½ cup shredded carrot

2 hard-cooked eggs, cut into wedges

Bring 4 cups *water* and 1 teaspoon *salt* to boiling. Add shrimp. Simmer, uncovered, for 1 to 3 minutes or till shrimp turn pink, stirring occasionally. Drain shrimp and rinse under cold running water. Cover and chill shrimp for 2 to 24 hours.

For dressing, in a small mixing bowl stir together mayonnaise or salad dressing, green onion, chili sauce, lemon peel, lemon juice, and horseradish. Cover and chill for 2 to 24 hours.

To serve, arrange tomato slices on 4 salad plates. Toss together shredded cabbage or romaine and shredded carrot; pile atop tomato slices. Top with chilled shrimp. Arrange egg wedges around each salad. Dollop dressing over salads. Makes 4 servings.

Time

Preparation	30 min.
Chilling	2 to 24 hrs.

Per Serving

Calories	348
Protein	20 g
Carbohydrate	12 g
Total Fat	26 g
Saturated Fat	4 g
Cholesterol	247 mg
Sodium	467 mg
Potassium	655 mg

The Perfect Hard-Cooked Egg

Have you ever gotten a greenish ring around the yolk of a hard-cooked egg? To minimize the chances of this harmless but unattractive ring forming, follow these directions.

Place the eggs in a saucepan and add enough cold water to come 1 inch above the eggs. Bring the water to boiling over high heat. Reduce the heat so the water is just below simmering. Cover and cook the eggs for 15 minutes; drain. Run *cold* water over the eggs or place them in ice water till they're cool enough to handle; drain.

To peel, gently tap each egg on the countertop. Roll the egg between the palms of your hands. Peel off the eggshell, starting at the large end.

SEVICHE SALAD

8 ounces fresh or frozen peeled and deveined shrimp

6 ounces fresh or frozen sea scallops

¾ cup lime juice or lemon juice

¼ cup sliced green onion (4 medium)

1 4-ounce can diced green chili peppers, drained

3 tablespoons olive oil or cooking oil

2 tablespoons snipped fresh cilantro or parsley

1 tablespoon capers, drained

¾ cup coarsely chopped, seeded tomato (1 medium)

Boston or Bibb lettuce leaves

1 avocado, seeded, peeled, and sliced (optional)

Lime wedges

Thaw shrimp and scallops, if frozen. Cut large scallops in half. Bring 4 cups *water* and 1 teaspoon *salt* to boiling. Add shrimp. Simmer, uncovered, for 1 minute. Add scallops. Simmer, uncovered, for 1 to 2 minutes more or till shrimp turn pink and scallops are opaque, stirring occasionally. Drain and rinse under cold running water.

❧

Place shrimp and scallops in a medium mixing bowl. Pour lime juice or lemon juice over shrimp and scallops. Cover and marinate for 4 to 24 hours, stirring occasionally. Drain shrimp and scallops, discarding marinade.

❧

In a medium mixing bowl stir together green onion, chili peppers, olive oil or cooking oil, cilantro or parsley, and capers. Gently stir in shrimp and scallops. Cover and chill for 30 minutes. Gently toss chopped tomato into seafood mixture.

❧

To serve, line 4 salad plates with lettuce leaves. Top with seafood mixture. If desired, arrange avocado slices around each salad. Garnish with lime wedges. Makes 4 servings.

Seviche usually refers to an appetizer of raw fish that's marinated in lime or lemon juice. For our salad version, we've opted to cook the seafood, but still marinate it in the citrus juice and toss it with the usual onions, peppers, and tomatoes.

Time

Preparation	15 min.
Marinating	4 to 24 hrs.
Assembling	40 min.

Per Serving

Calories	198
Protein	18 g
Carbohydrate	9 g
Total Fat	11 g
Saturated Fat	2 g
Cholesterol	97 mg
Sodium	481 mg
Potassium	412 mg

SCALLOP SALAD WITH FRUIT SALSA

This colorful, low-fat salad calls for large sea scallops. If you prefer, use the same weight of smaller bay scallops instead.

---

1 small pineapple (about 3 pounds)

1 cup strawberries, chopped

1 small ripe nectarine, pitted and chopped, **or** *peach, peeled, pitted, and chopped (¾ cup)*

2 jalapeño peppers, seeded and chopped (2 tablespoons)

1 to 2 tablespoons snipped fresh cilantro **or** *parsley*

Several dashes bottled hot pepper sauce

¼ cup orange juice

12 ounces fresh **or** *frozen sea scallops*

Boston **or** *Bibb lettuce leaves*

Use a sharp knife to cut two ¾-inch-thick crosswise slices from the center of the pineapple. Cut *each* slice into *six* wedges. Remove the hard core from each wedge. Wrap and refrigerate the pineapple wedges. Peel, core, and finely chop enough of the remaining pineapple to make ¾ cup (save the remaining pineapple for another use).

❦

For salsa, combine the ¾ cup chopped pineapple, strawberries, nectarine, jalapeño peppers, cilantro, and hot pepper sauce. Place about *1 cup* of the fruit mixture in a blender container or food processor bowl with orange juice. Cover and blend or process just till pureed. Stir into remaining fruit mixture. Cover and chill for several hours or overnight, stirring occasionally.

❦

Thaw scallops, if frozen. Cut large scallops in half. Bring 4 cups *water* and 1 teaspoon *salt* to boiling. Add scallops. Simmer, uncovered, 1 to 2 minutes or till scallops are opaque, stirring occasionally. Drain; rinse under cold running water. Cover; chill several hours or overnight.

❦

To serve, line 4 salad plates with lettuce leaves. Arrange *three* of the reserved pineapple wedges on *each* plate, pointing toward the center. Divide scallops among plates. Top with salsa. If desired, garnish each plate with sliced kiwi fruit and cilantro leaves. Makes 4 servings.

Time

Preparation	30 min.
Chilling	3 to 8 hrs.

Per Serving

Calories	120
Protein	15 g
Carbohydrate	13 g
Total Fat	1 g
Saturated Fat	0 g
Cholesterol	28 mg
Sodium	190 mg
Potassium	464 mg

Handle Hot Peppers Carefully

When seeding and chopping hot peppers such as the jalapeños in the recipe above, protect your hands with rubber gloves because the oils in the peppers can irritate your skin. Also, be careful not to touch or rub your eyes. When you're done handling the hot peppers, wash your hands and nails well with soap and water.

Use the tarragon
vinegar made
with white wine,
not red wine, so it
doesn't discolor
the salad dressing.
And if sorrel is
hard to come by,
use all spinach.

TOSSED SEAFOOD SALAD WITH TARRAGON-MUSTARD DRESSING

*12 ounces fresh **or** frozen peeled and deveined shrimp*

*8 ounces fresh **or** frozen scallops*

6 cups torn spinach

4 cups torn sorrel

1 cup frozen peas, thawed

½ cup sliced radishes

¼ cup sliced green onion (4 medium)

Tarragon-Mustard Dressing

Time

Preparation	*20 min.*
Chilling	*2 to 24 hrs.*

Per Serving

Calories	*274*
Protein	*22 g*
Carbohydrate	*12 g*
Total Fat	*18 g*
Saturated Fat	*3 g*
Cholesterol	*108 mg*
Sodium	*439 mg*
Potassium	*932 mg*

Thaw shrimp and scallops, if frozen. Bring 4 cups *water* and 1 teaspoon *salt* to boiling. Add shrimp. Simmer, uncovered, for 1 minute. Add scallops. Simmer, uncovered, for 1 to 2 minutes more or till shrimp turn pink and scallops are opaque, stirring occasionally. Drain and rinse under cold running water. Cover and chill for 2 to 24 hours.

❧

To serve, in a large salad bowl combine spinach, sorrel, peas, radishes, and green onion. Add shrimp and scallops. Pour dressing over salad. Toss lightly to coat. Makes 6 servings.

TARRAGON-MUSTARD DRESSING

In a small mixing bowl stir together ½ cup *mayonnaise or salad dressing;* 2 tablespoons *dairy sour cream;* 4 teaspoons *Dijon-style mustard;* 1 tablespoon snipped fresh *tarragon or* ½ teaspoon dried *tarragon,* crushed; and 1 tablespoon *white wine tarragon vinegar.*

LOBSTER-MELON SALAD

1 medium honeydew melon or cantaloupe

6 cups torn romaine

8 ounces coarsely flaked, cooked lobster or one 8-ounce package frozen, lobster-flavored, chunk-style fish pieces

1 medium papaya, seeded, peeled, and chopped (1½ cups)

2 tablespoons snipped chives

Orange Vinaigrette

Lettuce leaves

8 to 12 edible flowers (such as violas or pansies) (optional)

Cut honeydew melon or cantaloupe in half and remove the seeds. Use a melon baller to scoop out pulp (you should have about 3 cups of melon balls).

In a mixing bowl combine melon balls, romaine, lobster, papaya, and chives. Pour Orange Vinaigrette over the salad. Toss lightly to coat. Transfer to a lettuce-lined salad bowl. Garnish with edible flowers, if desired. Makes 4 servings.

ORANGE VINAIGRETTE

In a screw-top jar combine ¼ cup *salad oil,* 1 teaspoon finely shredded *orange peel,* ¼ cup *orange juice,* 1 tablespoon *Dijon-style mustard,* and ⅛ teaspoon *pepper.* Cover and shake well.

The lobster-flavored fish pieces sometimes are called surimi. This "seafood" is actually processed fish that has been flavored and re-formed to make imitation seafood products.

Time

Start to finish   25 min.

Per Serving

Calories	*375*
Protein	*16 g*
Carbohydrate	*41 g*
Total Fat	*20 g*
Saturated Fat	*2 g*
Cholesterol	*41 mg*
Sodium	*375 mg*
Potassium	*1,447 mg*

NO-FUSS
Main-Dish Salads

Some days you're just too busy to think about fixing meals. That's where the salad recipes in this chapter come in. Because each recipe requires only a few ingredients (usually five or fewer), mealtime preparation is fast and simple. More than half of these main-dish recipes can be on your table in about 20 minutes. Others can be quickly assembled one day and refrigerated so they're ready to eat the next. As you look through the next 11 pages, you'll be surprised at the variety of fast-paced salads you can create.

Time

Start to finish   20 min.

Per Serving

Calories	399
Protein	26 g
Carbohydrate	21 g
Total Fat	24 g
Saturated Fat	3 g
Cholesterol	60 mg
Sodium	376 mg
Potassium	996 mg

BEEF AND FRUIT SALAD

6 cups torn spinach **or** *torn mixed greens*

2 cups cubed cooked lean beef **or** *pork*

1 16-ounce can fruits for salad **or** *tropical fruit salad, chilled and drained*

1 medium cucumber, thinly sliced (1¾ cups)

½ cup bottled poppy seed salad dressing **or** *bottled creamy cucumber salad dressing*

In a large salad bowl combine torn spinach or mixed greens, cubed beef or pork, chilled fruit, and sliced cucumber. Pour desired salad dressing over salad. Toss lightly to coat. Serves 4.

DELI-MEAT-AND-BEAN SALAD

Time

Start to finish 20 min.

Per Serving

Calories	363
Protein	23 g
Carbohydrate	39 g
Total Fat	13 g
Saturated Fat	7 g
Cholesterol	52 mg
Sodium	676 mg
Potassium	389 mg

1 cup corkscrew macaroni or *wagon wheel macaroni*

4 cups torn iceberg lettuce or *torn mixed greens*

1 pint deli three-bean salad or *one 15- or 17- ounce can three-bean salad, chilled*

4 ounces cooked lean beef, turkey, or *ham, cut into bite-size strips (¾ cup)*

1 cup cubed cheddar, brick, provolone, or *Swiss cheese (4 ounces)*

Cook pasta according to package directions. Drain pasta. Transfer cooked pasta to a bowl of ice water. Let stand 5 minutes. Drain well.

❧

In a large salad bowl combine lettuce or mixed greens; *undrained* three-bean salad; beef, turkey, or ham strips; and cheese. Add chilled pasta. Toss lightly to mix. Makes 4 servings.

PEPPY TACO SALADS

Time

Start to finish 20 min.

Per Serving

Calories	319
Protein	25 g
Carbohydrate	7 g
Total Fat	22 g
Saturated Fat	11 g
Cholesterol	85 mg
Sodium	507 mg
Potassium	510 mg

¾ pound lean ground beef or *ground pork*

¾ cup salsa

8 cups torn iceberg lettuce or *torn mixed greens*

1 cup shredded Monterey Jack cheese with jalapeño peppers

or *shredded cheddar cheese (4 ounces)*

¼ cup dairy sour cream or *plain yogurt*

Tortilla chips (optional)

In a medium saucepan cook ground beef or ground pork till brown. Drain off fat. Stir in salsa and heat through.

❧

Place lettuce in a large salad bowl. Spoon meat mixture over lettuce. Sprinkle with shredded cheese. Toss lightly to mix. Dollop each serving with sour cream or yogurt. If desired, serve with tortilla chips. Makes 4 servings.

Time

Start to finish   15 min.

Per Serving

Calories	353
Protein	24 g
Carbohydrate	45 g
Total Fat	9 g
Saturated Fat	1 g
Cholesterol	46 mg
Sodium	515 mg
Potassium	649 mg

TUNA AND SLAW SALAD

1 pint deli coleslaw

1 9¼-ounce can chunk white tuna (water pack), chilled

1 8-ounce can pineapple chunks (juice pack), chilled and drained

1 cup chopped pear **or** *apple (1 medium)*

⅓ cup raisins

Shredded iceberg lettuce

If coleslaw is very wet, drain off excess liquid. Drain tuna and break into chunks.

❧

In a medium mixing bowl combine coleslaw, pineapple chunks, chopped pear or apple, and raisins. Arrange shredded lettuce on 4 salad plates. Spoon coleslaw mixture into the center of each plate. Make an indentation in the center of each mound of coleslaw mixture; fill with tuna chunks. Makes 4 servings.

Time

Start to finish   20 min.

Per Serving

Calories	381
Protein	27 g
Carbohydrate	10 g
Total Fat	26 g
Saturated Fat	6 g
Cholesterol	57 mg
Sodium	671 mg
Potassium	792 mg

TUNA-HAVARTI SALAD

1 9¼-ounce can chunk white tuna (water pack), chilled

6 cups torn spinach **or** *torn mixed greens*

2 cups sliced strawberries

1 cup cubed creamy Havarti **or** *Monterey Jack cheese (4 ounces)*

½ cup bottled creamy Parmesan salad dressing **or** *bottled creamy cucumber salad dressing*

Drain tuna and break into chunks. In a large salad bowl combine spinach or mixed greens, sliced strawberries, and cubed cheese; add tuna chunks. Pour salad dressing over salad. Toss lightly to coat. Makes 4 servings.

SALMON AND VEGETABLE SALAD

1½ cups frozen cut green beans

4 cups sliced cooked potatoes **or** *two 16-ounce cans sliced potatoes, chilled and drained*

¾ cup bottled creamy Parmesan salad dressing

Shredded iceberg lettuce

4 medium tomatoes, sliced

2 6½-ounce cans skinless boneless salmon, chilled, drained, and flaked

In a colander run water over frozen green beans just till thawed. In a mixing bowl combine green beans and potatoes. Pour the salad dressing over the vegetables. Toss lightly to coat. Arrange shredded lettuce on 4 salad plates. Arrange tomato slices around edges of plates. Spoon the vegetable mixture into the center of each plate. Top with salmon. Makes 4 servings.

Time

Start to finish   15 min.

Per Serving

Calories	553
Protein	23 g
Carbohydrate	62 g
Total Fat	24 g
Saturated Fat	1 g
Cholesterol	58 mg
Sodium	492 mg
Potassium	1,683 mg

CRAB-STUFFED PAPAYAS

2 large ripe papayas

2 cups red raspberries **or** *one 10-ounce package frozen red raspberries, thawed*

⅓ cup vanilla yogurt

1 12-ounce package frozen crabmeat, thawed, **or** *two 8-ounce packages frozen, crab-flavored, salad-style fish, thawed*

Shredded Boston **or** *Bibb lettuce*

¼ cup sliced almonds **or** *chopped pecans, toasted,* **or** *cashews*

Halve papayas lengthwise. Scoop out seeds; scoop out pulp, leaving a ½-inch-thick shell. Peel papaya. Brush shells with lemon juice. Chop enough pulp to measure ½ cup; set aside. If using frozen raspberries, drain off juice, reserving 1 to 2 tablespoons. Set juice aside.

❧

For dressing, in a mixing bowl stir 1 to 2 tablespoons *milk (or* reserved raspberry juice) into yogurt to desired consistency. Stir chopped papaya, raspberries, and crabmeat into dressing.

❧

Arrange lettuce on 4 salad plates. Spoon crab mixture into papaya shells. Place papaya shells on plates. Sprinkle each salad with nuts. Makes 4 servings.

Time

Start to finish   30 min.

Per Serving

Calories	275
Protein	21 g
Carbohydrate	39 g
Total Fat	5 g
Saturated Fat	1 g
Cholesterol	86 mg
Sodium	254 mg
Potassium	898 mg

Reduce the fat in this salad by 7 grams just by using our Low-Calorie Thousand Island Dressing (see recipe, page 215).

SEAFOOD SALAD WITH ORANGES

Chinese cabbage leaves

4 cups shredded romaine **or** iceberg lettuce

2 8-ounce packages frozen, crab-flavored, fish pieces, thawed and cut into 1-inch pieces, **or** two 8-ounce packages frozen, peeled, cooked shrimp, thawed

3 oranges, peeled and sectioned

1 small avocado, seeded, peeled, and sliced (optional)

¾ cup Thousand Island Dressing (see recipe, page 205) **or** bottled Thousand Island salad dressing

Orange slices (optional)

Lime slices (optional)

Fresh thyme (optional)

Time

Start to finish   35 min.

Line 4 salad plates with Chinese cabbage leaves. Pile shredded romaine or iceberg lettuce in the center of each plate.

❧

Place crab-flavored fish pieces or shrimp atop the shredded romaine. Arrange orange sections and, if desired, avocado slices on the side of each salad. Spoon dressing over salad. If desired, garnish with orange and lime slices and thyme. Makes 4 servings.

Per Serving

Calories	452
Protein	21 g
Carbohydrate	28 g
Total Fat	30 g
Saturated Fat	5 g
Cholesterol	76 mg
Sodium	475 mg
Potassium	810 mg

Time

Start to finish	20 min.

Per Serving

Calories	261
Protein	19 g
Carbohydrate	14 g
Total Fat	15 g
Saturated Fat	2 g
Cholesterol	145 mg
Sodium	184 mg
Potassium	490 mg

TOSSED ORIENTAL SALAD

12 ounces fresh **or** *frozen cooked shrimp*

6 cups torn mixed greens

1 8-ounce can sliced water chestnuts, drained

1 6-ounce package frozen pea pods, thawed

⅓ cup Ginger Vinaigrette (see recipe, page 211)

Thaw shrimp, if frozen. In a large salad bowl combine shrimp, mixed greens, water chestnuts, and pea pods. Pour the Ginger Vinaigrette over salad. Toss lightly to coat. Makes 4 servings.

Time

Preparation	60 min.
Chilling	4 to 24 hrs.

Per Serving

Calories	333
Protein	25 g
Carbohydrate	31 g
Total Fat	13 g
Saturated Fat	2 g
Cholesterol	166 mg
Sodium	368 mg
Potassium	490 mg

WILD RICE AND SHRIMP SALAD

12 ounces fresh **or** *frozen cooked shrimp*

1 cup wild rice

2 cups water

1 6½-ounce jar marinated artichoke hearts, drained

3 cups torn romaine **or** *torn spinach*

¼ cup Garlic Vinaigrette (see recipe, page 211)

Thaw shrimp, if frozen. Meanwhile, rinse the wild rice in a strainer under *cold* water about 1 minute. In a medium saucepan combine wild rice and the 2 cups water. Bring to boiling; reduce heat. Cover and simmer about 40 minutes or till rice is tender and liquid is absorbed. Cool rice slightly.

❧

Cut any large artichoke hearts in half. In a large mixing bowl combine shrimp, cooked rice, artichoke hearts, and romaine or spinach. Pour the Garlic Vinaigrette over the salad. Toss lightly to coat. Cover and chill for 4 to 24 hours. Makes 4 servings.

OH-SO-EASY CHEF'S SALAD

Time

Start to finish   20 min.

4 cups cut-up salad-bar vegetables (broccoli flowerets, cauliflower flowerets, sliced radishes, carrots, green pepper rings or strips, cucumber slices, fresh mushrooms, cherry tomatoes, or zucchini slices)

6 cups torn mixed greens or mesclun

4 ounces cooked turkey, ham, or lean beef, cut into thin strips

4 ounces thinly sliced Swiss, cheddar, provolone, brick, or creamy Havarti cheese, cut into bite-size strips or crumbled blue cheese

½ cup bottled oil-free Italian salad dressing or desired bottled salad dressing

Per Serving	
Calories	197
Protein	20 g
Carbohydrate	9 g
Total Fat	9 g
Saturated Fat	5 g
Cholesterol	46 mg
Sodium	532 mg
Potassium	553 mg

Cut up any large salad-bar vegetable pieces, if necessary. In a large salad bowl combine vegetables; mixed greens or mesclun; turkey, ham, or beef; and cheese. Pour desired salad dressing over salad. Toss lightly to coat. Makes 4 servings.

TURKEY AND FRUIT SALAD WITH CURRY DRESSING

Time

Start to finish   20 min.

½ cup Green Goddess Dressing (see recipe, page 207) or bottled Green Goddess salad dressing

1 to 1½ teaspoons curry powder

6 cups torn Bibb or Boston lettuce or torn mixed greens

10 ounces cooked turkey, cut into thin strips (2 cups)

1 6-ounce package mixed dried fruit bits

Per Serving	
Calories	334
Protein	25 g
Carbohydrate	35 g
Total Fat	12 g
Saturated Fat	3 g
Cholesterol	59 mg
Sodium	159 mg
Potassium	833 mg

For dressing, in a small mixing bowl stir together Green Goddess Dressing and curry powder. Set dressing aside.

In a large salad bowl combine lettuce or mixed greens, turkey, and dried fruit bits. Pour dressing over salad. Toss lightly to coat. Makes 4 servings.

CHICKEN-FILLED MELONS

Per Serving

Calories	248
Protein	25 g
Carbohydrate	29 g
Total Fat	4 g
Saturated Fat	1 g
Cholesterol	60 mg
Sodium	116 mg
Potassium	1,002 mg

2 small cantaloupes or honeydew melons

½ cup lemon yogurt or pineapple yogurt

1 tablespoon honey

2 cups cubed cooked chicken or turkey

1 cup bias-sliced celery (2 stalks)

Lettuce leaves

Cut melons in half and remove the seeds. Use a melon baller to scoop out the pulp. Chill *3 cups* of the melon balls till serving time (chill remaining melon balls for another use.) Trim a thin slice from the bottom of each melon shell. Set aside.

Combine yogurt and honey. Stir in the reserved 3 cups of melon balls, chicken, and celery. Line each melon shell with lettuce leaves. Spoon chicken mixture into melon shells. Serves 4.

GREEK-STYLE CHICKEN SALAD IN TOMATO TULIPS

Per Serving

Calories	263
Protein	20 g
Carbohydrate	10 g
Total Fat	17 g
Saturated Fat	4 g
Cholesterol	57 mg
Sodium	383 mg
Potassium	462 mg

4 large tomatoes

1½ cups cubed cooked chicken or turkey

½ cup crumbled feta cheese (2 ounces)

½ cup sliced pitted ripe olives

⅓ cup Walnut Vinaigrette (see recipe, page 209)

Shredded iceberg lettuce

For tomato tulips, cut out ½ inch of the core from each tomato. Invert tomatoes. Cutting from the top to, *but not through,* the stem end, cut each tomato into 6 wedges. Set aside.

Combine chicken, feta cheese, and ripe olives. Pour the Walnut Vinaigrette over the chicken mixture. Toss lightly to coat. Arrange shredded lettuce on 4 salad plates. Place tomatoes atop lettuce. Spread tomato wedges slightly apart; fill with the chicken mixture. Makes 4 servings.

FRIED CHICKEN AND SPINACH SALAD

1 12-ounce package frozen breaded small chunk-shape chicken patties

6 cups torn spinach or torn mixed greens

16 cherry tomatoes, halved

¼ cup grated Parmesan cheese

⅓ cup desired bottled creamy salad dressing

Place the frozen chicken patties on a baking sheet. Bake in a 400° oven for 7 to 10 minutes or till done. Cut each patty in half crosswise.

⁂

In a large salad bowl combine torn spinach and cherry tomatoes. Sprinkle with Parmesan cheese. Add chicken pieces. Pour dressing over salad. Toss lightly to coat. Makes 4 servings.

Time

Start to finish	25 min.

Per Serving

Calories	371
Protein	18 g
Carbohydrate	17 g
Total Fat	27 g
Saturated Fat	1 g
Cholesterol	40 mg
Sodium	850 mg
Potassium	580 mg

TURKEY AND VEGETABLE SALAD

1 pound whole tiny new potatoes, quartered

3 cups loose-pack frozen broccoli, French-style green beans, onions, and red pepper

2 cups cubed cooked turkey or chicken

½ cup bottled Italian salad dressing

Iceberg lettuce leaves

¼ cup grated Parmesan cheese

In a covered saucepan cook potatoes in boiling salted water for 12 to 15 minutes or till just tender. Drain; cool slightly. Meanwhile, in a colander run water over frozen vegetables to separate pieces.

⁂

In a large mixing bowl combine potatoes, vegetables, and turkey or chicken. Pour salad dressing over salad. Toss lightly to coat. Cover and chill for 4 to 24 hours.

⁂

Line 4 salad plates with lettuce leaves. Spoon salad atop lettuce. Sprinkle with Parmesan cheese. Makes 4 servings.

Time

Preparation	35 min.
Chilling	4 to 24 hrs.

Per Serving

Calories	418
Protein	28 g
Carbohydrate	36 g
Total Fat	22 g
Saturated Fat	4 g
Cholesterol	52 mg
Sodium	392 mg
Potassium	761 mg

PINEAPPLE-HAM SALAD

Time

Preparation	20 min.
Chilling	4 to 24 hrs.

Per Serving

Calories	395
Protein	20 g
Carbohydrate	31 g
Total Fat	23 g
Saturated Fat	3 g
Cholesterol	39 mg
Sodium	944 mg
Potassium	545 mg

10 ounces fully cooked lean ham **or** *pork, cut into julienne strips (2 cups)*

1 15¼-ounce can pineapple tidbits (juice pack), drained, **or** *one 15-ounce can mandarin orange sections, drained*

1 cup seedless green **or** *red grapes, halved*

¾ cup broken pecans, toasted

⅓ cup Cranberry-Mint Vinaigrette (see recipe, page 210) **or** *Citrus and Poppy Seed Vinaigrette (see recipe, page 211)*

Shredded iceberg lettuce

In a large mixing bowl combine ham or pork strips, pineapple tidbits or mandarin oranges, grapes, and toasted pecans. Pour the Cranberry-Mint Vinaigrette or Citrus and Poppy Seed Vinaigrette over salad. Toss lightly to coat. Cover and chill for 4 to 24 hours.

❧

Arrange shredded lettuce on 4 salad plates. Spoon salad atop lettuce. Makes 4 servings.

SALAMI-POTATO SALAD PLATE

Time

Start to finish	20 min.

Per Serving

Calories	642
Protein	24 g
Carbohydrate	32 g
Total Fat	43 g
Saturated Fat	16 g
Cholesterol	238 mg
Sodium	2,034 mg
Potassium	934 mg

Romaine leaves

1 tablespoon snipped fresh dill **or** *1 teaspoon dried dillweed*

1 quart deli mayonnaise-style potato salad

1¾ cup thinly sliced zucchini **or** *cucumber (1 medium)*

6 ounces sliced salami, cut into strips

8 round slices Colby cheese, halved (about 6 ounces)

Fresh dill (optional)

Line 4 salad plates with romaine leaves. Stir dill into potato salad. Spoon potato salad atop romaine. Arrange the zucchini or cucumber slices, salami, and cheese around the potato salad. If desired, garnish with dill. Makes 4 servings.

RIGATONI AND HAM SALAD

1 cup rigatoni **or** *mostaccioli (about 3½ ounces)*

1 16-ounce package loose-pack frozen broccoli, cauliflower, and carrots

6 ounces fully cooked lean ham **or** *smoked turkey, cut into julienne strips (1¼ cups)*

1 cup cubed provolone **or** *Swiss cheese (4 ounces)*

⅓ cup bottled Italian salad dressing

Romaine leaves **or** *iceberg lettuce leaves*

Cook pasta according to package directions, omitting salt. Drain pasta. Rinse with *cold* water; drain again. Meanwhile, in a colander run water over frozen vegetables to separate pieces. In a large mixing bowl combine pasta, vegetables, ham or turkey, and cheese. Pour salad dressing over pasta mixture. Toss lightly to coat. Cover and chill for 4 to 24 hours.

❧

Line 4 salad plates with romaine leaves. Spoon salad atop romaine leaves. Serves 4.

Time

Preparation	25 min.
Chilling	4 to 24 hrs.

Per Serving

Calories	401
Protein	24 g
Carbohydrate	32 g
Total Fat	22 g
Saturated Fat	7 g
Cholesterol	43 mg
Sodium	1,011 mg
Potassium	510 mg

CREAMY HAM AND RICE SALAD

⅔ cup long grain rice

3 cups loose-pack frozen zucchini, carrots, cauliflower, lima beans, and Italian beans **or** *loose-pack frozen cauliflower, broccoli, and carrots*

10 ounces cubed fully cooked lean ham **or** *pork (2 cups)*

½ cup bias-sliced celery (1 stalk)

¾ cup bottled creamy Italian salad dressing **or** *bottled blue cheese salad dressing*

Boston **or** *Bibb lettuce leaves*

Cook rice according to package directions. Cool rice slightly. Meanwhile, in a colander run water over frozen vegetables to separate pieces. In a large mixing bowl combine cooked rice, vegetables, ham or pork, and celery. Pour salad dressing over salad. Toss lightly to coat. Cover and chill for 4 to 24 hours.

❧

Line 4 salad plates with lettuce leaves. Before serving, if necessary, stir 1 to 2 tablespoons *milk* into salad to moisten. Spoon salad atop lettuce. Makes 4 servings.

Time

Preparation	15 min.
Chilling	4 to 24 hrs.

Per Serving

Calories	369
Protein	24 g
Carbohydrate	45 g
Total Fat	10 g
Saturated Fat	1 g
Cholesterol	39 mg
Sodium	1,342 mg
Potassium	669 mg

Side-Dish Salads

From pasta to potato, molded to marinated, and all the other options in between, this vast collection of tantalizing side salads is sure to please. With the dozens of intriguing combinations in this chapter, you're bound to find just the right one to play a supporting role at your next meal.

TOSSED GREENS WITH NASTURTIUMS

The bright red, yellow, and orange shades of nasturtium petals make this salad as wonderful to look at as it is to eat. What's more, the petals give this dish a slight peppery flavor.

¼ cup salad oil

2 tablespoons water

2 tablespoons lemon juice

2 tablespoons sliced green onion (2 medium)

1 teaspoon sugar

1 teaspoon Dijon-style mustard

⅛ teaspoon pepper

1 clove garlic, minced

2 cups torn spinach

*1 cup torn Boston **or** Bibb lettuce*

1 cup torn red-tip leaf lettuce

1 cup watercress (2 ounces)

1 cup sliced fresh mushrooms

*12 nasturtium flowers **or** other edible flowers*

Time

Start to finish   20 min.

For dressing, in a screw-top jar combine oil, water, lemon juice, green onion, sugar, mustard, pepper, and garlic. Cover and shake well.

⚜

In a large bowl combine spinach, Boston or Bibb lettuce, red-tip leaf lettuce, watercress, and sliced mushrooms. Shake dressing well; pour over salad. Toss lightly to coat. Divide salad among 4 salad plates. Top each serving with nasturtium flowers. Makes 4 servings.

Per Serving

Calories	116
Protein	2 g
Carbohydrate	5 g
Total Fat	11 g
Saturated Fat	1 g
Cholesterol	0 mg
Sodium	68 mg
Potassium	329 mg

Members of our taste panel suggested using vinegar flavored with tarragon, chives, or basil in the creamy horseradish dressing.

Time

Start to finish 25 min.

Per Serving

Calories	126
Protein	10 g
Carbohydrate	10 g
Total Fat	5 g
Saturated Fat	3 g
Cholesterol	13 mg
Sodium	385 mg
Potassium	460 mg

COTTAGE CHEESE AND SPINACH SALAD

½ cup dairy sour cream

2 tablespoons sugar

1 tablespoon prepared horseradish

½ teaspoon dry mustard

¼ teaspoon salt

3 tablespoons herb-flavored vinegar

7 cups torn spinach

1½ cups low-fat cottage cheese

½ cup coarsely chopped walnuts (optional)

For dressing, in a small mixing bowl stir together sour cream, sugar, prepared horseradish, dry mustard, and salt. Using a wire whisk, gradually mix in the herb-flavored vinegar. Cover and chill till serving time.

❧

To serve, place the torn spinach in a large salad bowl. Spoon the cottage cheese on top of the spinach in a ring. Sprinkle with the walnuts, if desired. Pour dressing over salad. Toss lightly to coat. Makes 6 to 8 servings.

SANTA FE SALAD

2 tablespoons salad oil

2 tablespoons vinegar

1 teaspoon sugar

1 clove garlic, minced

Dash bottled hot pepper sauce

5 cups torn mixed greens

1 avocado, seeded, peeled, and sliced

1 8-ounce can red kidney beans, rinsed and drained

½ cup coarsely chopped, seeded tomato (1 small)

2 tablespoons pumpkin seed **or** pine nuts, toasted (optional)

For dressing, in a screw-top jar combine oil, vinegar, sugar, garlic, and bottled hot pepper sauce. Cover and shake well.

❧

In a large salad bowl combine mixed greens, avocado slices, kidney beans, and chopped tomato. Shake dressing well; pour over salad. Toss lightly to coat. Sprinkle with pumpkin seed or pine nuts, if desired. Makes 6 servings.

The cooling flavor of avocado, teamed with the peppery vinaigrette, gives this salad a southwestern flavor.

Time

Start to finish   24 min.

Per Serving

Calories	151
Protein	5 g
Carbohydrate	11 g
Total Fat	11 g
Saturated Fat	2 g
Cholesterol	0 mg
Sodium	81 mg
Potassium	445 mg

The tart, lemony flavor of sorrel makes this a great salad for a fish dinner.

WILTED SORREL SALAD

4 slices bacon

1 small red onion, sliced and separated into rings

2 tablespoons dry sherry

2 tablespoons honey

*8 cups torn sorrel **and/or** spinach*

*Violets, pansies, **or** other edible flowers (optional)*

In a large skillet cook bacon over medium heat till crisp. Remove bacon, reserving *2 tablespoons* drippings in the skillet. Drain bacon on paper towels. Crumble bacon and set aside. Add onion to the reserved drippings in the skillet. Cook over medium heat till onion is tender but not brown. Stir in sherry and honey. Bring to boiling.

❧

Add sorrel and/or spinach to skillet. Toss for 30 to 60 seconds or till sorrel and spinach are just wilted. Transfer to a serving bowl. Garnish with flowers, if desired. Serve immediately. Makes 4 servings.

Time

Start to finish   20 min.

Per Serving

Calories	146
Protein	8 g
Carbohydrate	20 g
Total Fat	5 g
Saturated Fat	1 g
Cholesterol	5 mg
Sodium	113 mg
Potassium	1,125 mg

SESAME VEGETABLE SALAD

8 cups torn leaf lettuce

2 tablespoons sesame seed, toasted

¼ teaspoon sugar

⅓ cup dairy sour cream

⅓ cup mayonnaise or salad dressing

1 tablespoon vinegar

⅓ cup green pepper strips (½ of a small)

⅓ cup sliced cucumber (½ of a small)

⅓ cup bias-sliced carrot (1 small)

¼ cup finely chopped onion (½ of a medium)

Place lettuce in the bottom of a large salad bowl. Sprinkle with *1 tablespoon* of the toasted sesame seed and the sugar. Season with salt and pepper.

⚜

For dressing, in a small mixing bowl stir together sour cream, mayonnaise or salad dressing, and vinegar. Stir in green pepper, cucumber, carrot, and onion. Spread the dressing evenly over the top of the salad. Sprinkle with the remaining toasted sesame seed. Cover tightly with clear plastic wrap. Chill for 4 to 24 hours.

⚜

To serve, toss lightly to coat. Makes 8 servings.

To reduce the fat to 3 grams per serving, switch the sour cream to plain nonfat yogurt and use reduced-calorie mayonnaise or salad dressing. Fat-free mayonnaise or salad dressing reduces the fat even more.

Time

Start to finish	*20 min.*
Chilling	*4 to 24 hrs.*

Per Serving

Calories	*117*
Protein	*2 g*
Carbohydrate	*5 g*
Total Fat	*11 g*
Saturated Fat	*3 g*
Cholesterol	*10 mg*
Sodium	*65 mg*
Potassium	*224 mg*

ASPARAGUS AND WILTED GREENS

2 cups asparagus cut into 2-inch pieces (about ¾ pound)

4 slices bacon

1 small onion, sliced and separated into rings

2 tablespoons vinegar

1 tablespoon sugar

½ teaspoon fines herbes, crushed

⅛ teaspoon salt

1 cup torn Boston or Bibb lettuce

1 cup torn kale or 1½ cups torn sorrel

½ cup coarsely chopped, seeded tomato (1 small)

Time

Start to finish   25 min.

Per Serving

Calories	85
Protein	5 g
Carbohydrate	10 g
Total Fat	4 g
Saturated Fat	1 g
Cholesterol	5 mg
Sodium	180 mg
Potassium	436 mg

In a medium saucepan cook asparagus, covered, in a small amount of boiling water for 4 to 8 minutes or till crisp-tender. Drain.

✤

Meanwhile, in a large skillet cook bacon over medium heat till crisp. Remove bacon, reserving drippings in skillet. Drain bacon on paper towels. Crumble bacon and set aside. Add onion to reserved drippings in the skillet. Cook over medium heat till onion is tender but not brown. Stir in vinegar, sugar, fines herbes, and salt. Bring to boiling.

✤

Add asparagus, bacon, Boston or Bibb lettuce, kale or sorrel, and tomato to skillet. Toss for 30 to 60 seconds or till the greens are just wilted. Transfer to a serving bowl. Serve immediately. Makes 4 servings.

Orange and Avocado Salad With Tarragon Dressing

4 cups torn mixed greens

1 11-ounce can mandarin orange sections, drained

1 cup sliced fresh mushrooms

½ of a medium avocado, seeded, peeled, and cubed

½ cup shredded carrot (1 medium)

Tarragon Dressing

¼ cup slivered almonds **or** *pine nuts, toasted (optional)*

In a large salad bowl combine torn mixed greens, mandarin orange sections, mushrooms, avocado, and carrot. Pour Tarragon Dressing over salad. Toss lightly to coat. Sprinkle with almonds or pine nuts, if desired. Makes 6 to 8 servings.

Tarragon Dressing

In a small mixing bowl stir together ½ cup *mayonnaise or salad dressing;* 2 tablespoons *lemon juice or vinegar;* 1½ teaspoons *soy sauce;* 1 tablespoon snipped fresh *tarragon or* ½ teaspoon dried *tarragon,* crushed; ¼ teaspoon *pepper;* and 1 clove *garlic,* minced. Cover and chill till serving time. Makes about ⅔ cup.

Look for fresh mandarin oranges from January to May. If you find some, peel and section two or three, and add them to the salad instead of canned ones.

Time

Start to finish   27 min.

Per Serving

Calories	*200*
Protein	*2 g*
Carbohydrate	*12 g*
Total Fat	*17 g*
Saturated Fat	*3 g*
Cholesterol	*11 mg*
Sodium	*201 mg*
Potassium	*310 mg*

Blueberries aren't just for dessert anymore. They play a new role in the sweet, yet tart dressing of this savory salad.

GARDEN GREENS WITH HERBED BLUEBERRY VINAIGRETTE

4 cups torn mixed greens

1 cup sliced fresh mushrooms

2 medium apples, cored and sliced

½ cup Parmesan Croutons (see recipe, page 231)

½ cup Herbed Blueberry Vinaigrette

Fresh basil (optional)

In a large mixing bowl combine torn mixed greens and mushrooms. Toss lightly to mix. Divide salad among 4 salad plates. Top each plate with apple slices and Parmesan Croutons.

Shake Herbed Blueberry Vinaigrette well; pour about *2 tablespoons* of the vinaigrette over *each* salad. Makes 4 servings.

HERBED BLUEBERRY VINAIGRETTE

In a blender container or food processor bowl combine ½ cup fresh *or* frozen *blueberries* (thaw blueberries, if frozen), ¼ cup *white wine vinegar,* ½ teaspoon *sugar,* ⅛ teaspoon *pepper,* and dash *salt.* Cover and blend or process till the blueberries are puréed. Sieve the mixture to remove the skins; discard the skins. In a screw-top jar combine the blueberry mixture; 3 tablespoons *salad oil;* and 2 teaspoons snipped fresh *basil or* ½ teaspoon dried *basil,* crushed. Cover and shake well. Chill at least 1 hour. Store remaining dressing in the refrigerator for up to 2 weeks. Makes about 1⅓ cups.

Time

Preparation	20 min.
Chilling	1 hr.

Per Serving

Calories	131
Protein	2 g
Carbohydrate	18 g
Total Fat	7 g
Saturated Fat	3 g
Cholesterol	9 mg
Sodium	117 mg
Potassium	229 mg

Dijon-style mustard packs a flavor punch in this tangy sour cream dressing.

CUCUMBER AND ONION SALAD

1¾ cups thinly sliced cucumber (1 medium)

1 small red onion, sliced and separated into rings

½ cup dairy sour cream

2 teaspoons sugar

2 teaspoons tarragon vinegar or vinegar

½ teaspoon Dijon-style mustard

¼ teaspoon salt

⅛ teaspoon pepper

Time

Preparation	10 min.
Marinating	1 hr.

Per Serving

Calories	85
Protein	2 g
Carbohydrate	7 g
Total Fat	6 g
Saturated Fat	4 g
Cholesterol	13 mg
Sodium	170 mg
Potassium	162 mg

In a large mixing bowl combine cucumber slices and onion rings.

For marinade, in a small mixing bowl stir together sour cream, sugar, vinegar, mustard, salt, and pepper. Pour marinade over cucumber slices and onion rings. Toss lightly to coat. Cover and chill for up to 1 hour. Stir salad before serving. Makes 4 to 6 servings.

ANTIPASTO TRAY

2 cups cauliflower flowerets

1 small yellow summer squash **or** *zucchini, bias-sliced into ¼-inch-thick slices (about 1 cup)*

1 cup red **and/or** *yellow baby pear tomatoes* **or** *cherry tomatoes, halved*

1 4½-ounce jar whole mushrooms, drained

1 3½-ounce can pitted ripe olives, drained

Italian Vinaigrette (see recipe, page 211)

Romaine leaves

2 ounces thinly sliced salami **or** *ham*

2 ounces Colby, cheddar, provolone, **or** *mozzarella cheese, cut into sticks*

In a covered large saucepan cook cauliflower in a small amount of boiling water for 2 minutes. Add summer squash or zucchini; cook about 2 minutes more or till vegetables are nearly tender. Drain vegetables and cool slightly.

꙳

In a large mixing bowl combine cooked vegetables with tomatoes, mushrooms, and olives. Pour Italian Vinaigrette over vegetable mixture. Toss lightly to coat. Cover and chill for 4 to 24 hours, stirring occasionally.

꙳

To serve, line a serving platter with romaine leaves. Fold salami or ham slices in half; arrange salami or ham and cheese sticks in center of platter. Using a slotted spoon, transfer the vegetable mixture from marinade and arrange around the edge of the platter. Discard the marinade. Makes 6 servings.

If you're watching fat, substitute Oil-Free Dressing (see recipe, page 213) for the vinaigrette and thinly sliced chicken or turkey breast for the salami. Use low-fat cheese, too, and skip the olives.

Time

Preparation	20 min.
Marinating	4 to 24 hrs.

Per Serving

Calories	217
Protein	5 g
Carbohydrate	9 g
Total Fat	19 g
Saturated Fat	4 g
Cholesterol	15 mg
Sodium	374 mg
Potassium	309 mg

ROASTED PEPPER SALAD

Next time try artichoke hearts in place of the hearts of palm.

2 medium sweet red and/or yellow peppers

1 medium green pepper

1 cup broccoli flowerets

1 cup red and/or yellow baby pear tomatoes or cherry tomatoes, halved

½ cup sliced canned hearts of palm, drained

½ cup pitted ripe olives (optional)

2 tablespoons olive oil or salad oil

1 tablespoon snipped fresh basil or 1 teaspoon dried basil, crushed

1 tablespoon snipped parsley

1 tablespoon water

1 tablespoon lemon juice

2 cloves garlic, minced

Boston or Bibb lettuce leaves

Time

Preparation	50 min.
Marinating	4 to 24 hrs.

Per Serving

Calories	77
Protein	2 g
Carbohydrate	8 g
Total Fat	5 g
Saturated Fat	1 g
Cholesterol	0 mg
Sodium	44 mg
Potassium	327 mg

To roast peppers, quarter the peppers lengthwise. Remove the stems and seeds. Cut small slits into the ends of the pepper pieces to make them lie flat. Place pepper pieces, cut sides down, on a foil-lined baking sheet. Bake in a 425° oven for 20 to 25 minutes or till skins are bubbly and brown. Immediately place pepper pieces in a clean brown paper bag. Close bag tightly; cool.

Meanwhile, in a covered medium saucepan cook broccoli in a small amount of boiling water for 5 minutes; drain well.

Peel the cooled pepper pieces with a sharp knife. Cut lengthwise into ½-inch-wide strips; cut strips crosswise in half. In a large mixing bowl combine pepper strips, broccoli, tomatoes, hearts of palm, and, if desired, olives.

For marinade, in a screw-top jar combine oil, basil, parsley, water, lemon juice, garlic, ⅛ teaspoon *salt,* and ⅛ teaspoon *pepper.* Cover and shake well. Pour marinade over pepper mixture. Toss lightly to coat. Cover and chill for 4 to 24 hours, stirring occasionally.

To serve, line salad plates with lettuce leaves. Divide pepper mixture among the lettuce-lined plates. Makes 4 to 6 servings.

MARINATED CHEESE

8 ounces Monterey Jack **or** *mozzarella cheese*

1 medium sweet red, green, **or** *yellow pepper, cut into bite-size pieces (1 cup)*

1 6-ounce can pitted ripe jumbo olives, drained

⅓ cup olive oil **or** *salad oil*

⅓ cup white wine vinegar **or** *white vinegar*

1½ teaspoons dried Italian seasoning, crushed

½ teaspoon crushed red pepper

1 clove garlic, quartered

Cut the cheese into ½-inch cubes. (You should have about 2 cups.) Place the cheese cubes, sweet pepper, and olives in a 1½- to 2-quart container with a tight-fitting lid. Set aside.

❧

For marinade, in a small saucepan stir together olive oil or salad oil, vinegar, Italian seasoning, crushed red pepper, and garlic. Cook and stir just till heated through. Remove from heat; cool to room temperature. Pour the marinade over the cheese mixture in the container; stir to coat. Cover and chill in the refrigerator for 1 to 3 days, stirring occasionally.

❧

To serve, let the mixture stand at room temperature about 30 minutes. Using a slotted spoon, transfer cheese mixture to a small serving bowl. Discard garlic. Serve as a salad accompaniment. Return any remaining cheese mixture to marinade. Cover and chill up to 1 week. Bring to room temperature before serving. Makes 12 servings.

Transform a tossed salad into an Italian specialty by topping it with this zesty cheese-pepper-olive combo.

Time

Preparation	15 min.
Marinating	24 hrs.

Per Serving

Calories	127
Protein	5 g
Carbohydrate	2 g
Total Fat	12 g
Saturated Fat	4 g
Cholesterol	17 mg
Sodium	206 mg
Potassium	35 mg

Braised garlic gives a nutty, sweet taste to the herb dressing.

TOMATO WEDGES WITH BRAISED GARLIC MARINADE

4 or 5 large cloves garlic

1 teaspoon margarine or butter

¼ cup salad oil

¼ cup white wine vinegar or white vinegar

2 tablespoons thinly sliced green onion (2 medium)

1 tablespoon snipped fresh dill or 1 teaspoon dried dillweed

1 tablespoon snipped fresh basil or 1 teaspoon dried basil, crushed

1 tablespoon mayonnaise or salad dressing

¼ teaspoon salt

⅛ teaspoon pepper

4 medium tomatoes, cut into wedges

Leaf lettuce

Time

Preparation	20 min.
Marinating	2 to 4 hrs.

Per Serving

Calories	94
Protein	1 g
Carbohydrate	7 g
Total Fat	7 g
Saturated Fat	1 g
Cholesterol	1 mg
Sodium	81 mg
Potassium	326 mg

To braise garlic, in a covered small saucepan cook garlic cloves in hot margarine or butter over low heat about 15 minutes or till golden and soft, stirring frequently. Remove from heat and mash with a fork till the garlic is well combined with the margarine or butter.

❧

For marinade, in a screw-top jar combine braised garlic, oil, vinegar, green onion, dill, basil, mayonnaise or salad dressing, salt, and pepper. Cover and shake well.

❧

Place tomato wedges in a large mixing bowl. Pour marinade over tomato wedges. Cover and chill for 2 to 4 hours, stirring occasionally.

❧

To serve, line a salad bowl with lettuce leaves. Using a slotted spoon, transfer tomato wedges from marinade to lettuce-lined bowl. Discard remaining marinade. Makes 4 to 6 servings.

SUNRISE SALAD

2 sweet yellow peppers, cut into rings

½ teaspoon finely shredded orange peel

3 tablespoons orange juice

2 teaspoons snipped fresh chives

½ teaspoon honey

⅛ teaspoon salt

⅛ teaspoon freshly ground pepper

Lettuce leaves

6 to 9 plum tomatoes **or** 2 to 3 medium tomatoes, sliced

1 medium orange, sliced

1 cup red cherry tomatoes, halved

½ cup yellow cherry tomatoes, halved (optional)

Freshly ground pepper (optional)

In a covered large skillet cook yellow pepper rings in a small amount of boiling water for 1 to 2 minutes or till crisp-tender; drain and cool.

❦

For marinade, in a small mixing bowl stir together orange peel, orange juice, chives, honey, salt, and the ⅛ teaspoon pepper. Set aside.

❦

Place pepper rings in a plastic bag set in a bowl. Add marinade; close bag. Rotate bag to coat pepper rings with marinade. Chill for 4 to 24 hours, turning bag occasionally.

❦

To serve, line a large platter with lettuce leaves. Arrange tomato and orange slices around the edge of the platter. Drain pepper rings, reserving marinade. Arrange pepper rings in an overlapping circle inside tomato and orange slices. Fill center with red cherry tomatoes. If desired, garnish with yellow cherry tomatoes and sprinkle with additional pepper. Drizzle with reserved marinade. Makes 4 to 6 servings.

We named this salad for the red and yellow fruits and vegetables that you arrange on a platter to look like the sun.

Time

Preparation	15 min.
Marinating	4 to 24 hrs.
Assembling	15 min.

Per Serving

Calories	55
Protein	2 g
Carbohydrate	13 g
Total Fat	0 g
Saturated Fat	0 g
Cholesterol	0 mg
Sodium	77 mg
Potassium	384 mg

Chèvres vary in consistency. If you buy a firm chèvre, slice it into rounds. Pat softer chèvre into rounds with your hands.

MARINATED CHÈVRE

8 ounces chèvre cheese (goat cheese)

3 tablespoons olive oil or salad oil

1 tablespoon snipped fresh thyme or ½ teaspoon dried thyme, crushed

¼ teaspoon pepper

3 tablespoons fine dry bread crumbs

2 cups torn radicchio or shredded red cabbage

2 cups baby spinach or torn spinach

¼ cup Basic Vinaigrette (see recipe, page 211)

½ cup snipped parsley

4 small bunches red grapes

4 violas or other edible flowers (optional)

Time

| Preparation | 15 min. |
| Marinating | 30 min. |

Per Serving

Calories	344
Protein	16 g
Carbohydrate	13 g
Total Fat	26 g
Saturated Fat	1 g
Cholesterol	57 mg
Sodium	314 mg
Potassium	283 mg

Cut or shape chèvre into eight ½-inch-thick rounds. Place cheese rounds in a shallow dish. For marinade, stir together olive oil or salad oil, thyme, and pepper. Pour marinade over cheese. Let stand for 30 minutes, spooning marinade over cheese occasionally.

Remove cheese rounds from marinade; discard marinade. Pat bread crumbs onto both sides of cheese rounds. Place on a baking sheet. Bake in a 425° oven for 4 to 5 minutes or till cheese is slightly softened and crumbs are golden.

Meanwhile, in a large mixing bowl combine radicchio or red cabbage and spinach. Pour Basic Vinaigrette over greens. Toss lightly to coat. Divide greens among 4 salad plates.

Top each salad plate with two cheese rounds. Sprinkle half of the top of each cheese round with parsley. Add a bunch of grapes to each plate. Top with violas or other edible flowers, if desired. Serve immediately. Makes 4 servings.

MARINATED MUSHROOM SALAD

For a reduced-fat version, replace the olives with bite-size green or sweet red pepper strips and the marinade with Oil-Free Dressing (see recipe, page 213).

4½ cups sliced fresh mushrooms (12 ounces)

½ cup pitted ripe olives, halved

½ cup olive oil or salad oil

⅓ cup wine vinegar

2 tablespoons Dijon-style mustard

1½ teaspoons snipped fresh oregano or ½ teaspoon dried oregano, crushed

¼ teaspoon pepper

⅛ teaspoon salt

4 Boston or Bibb lettuce leaves

Watercress (optional)

Tomato slices (optional)

Time

Preparation	15 min.
Marinating	4 to 24 hrs.

Per Serving

Calories	88
Protein	2 g
Carbohydrate	6 g
Total Fat	7 g
Saturated Fat	1 g
Cholesterol	0 mg
Sodium	190 mg
Potassium	340 mg

In a large mixing bowl combine sliced mushrooms and olives.

For marinade, in a screw-top jar combine oil, vinegar, mustard, oregano, pepper, and salt. Cover and shake well. Pour marinade over mushroom and olive mixture. Cover and chill for 4 to 24 hours, stirring occasionally.

To serve, line 4 salad plates with Boston or Bibb lettuce leaves. If desired, arrange watercress and sliced tomatoes on the plates. Using a slotted spoon, divide mushroom and olive mixture among the plates. Discard marinade. Makes 4 servings.

CORN AND BEAN SALAD

Serve this Mexican-flavored salad at a summertime cookout instead of baked beans.

1 15-ounce can cannellini beans **or** *great northern beans, rinsed and drained*

1 15-ounce can black beans, rinsed and drained

1 8-ounce can whole kernel corn, drained

½ cup chopped green pepper (1 small)

¼ cup chopped red onion (1 small)

¼ cup salad oil

¼ cup vinegar

1 clove garlic, minced

2 tablespoons snipped fresh cilantro

2 tablespoons lime juice

1 tablespoon sugar

1 teaspoon chili powder

1 teaspoon ground cumin

¼ teaspoon salt

Lettuce leaves

In a large mixing bowl combine cannellini beans or great northern beans, black beans, corn, green pepper, and onion.

For marinade, in a screw-top jar combine oil, vinegar, garlic, cilantro, lime juice, sugar, chili powder, cumin, and salt. Cover and shake well. Pour marinade over vegetables. Toss lightly to coat. Cover and chill for 4 to 24 hours, stirring occasionally.

To serve, line a salad bowl with lettuce leaves. Using a slotted spoon, transfer vegetables from marinade to the lettuce-lined bowl. Discard marinade. Makes 6 servings.

Time

Preparation	10 min.
Marinating	4 to 24 hrs.

Per Serving

Calories	214
Protein	10 g
Carbohydrate	31 g
Total Fat	7 g
Saturated Fat	1 g
Cholesterol	0 mg
Sodium	218 mg
Potassium	484 mg

Freeze the extra pesto in an air-tight container for up to a month. Or chill it for a couple of days and toss it with some hot, cooked linguine. Whichever way you use it, bring it to room temperature before serving.

Time

Preparation	25 min.
Chilling	4 to 24 hrs.

Per Serving

Calories	216
Protein	5 g
Carbohydrate	19 g
Total Fat	14 g
Saturated Fat	2 g
Cholesterol	1 mg
Sodium	49 mg
Potassium	234 mg

PESTO PASTA SALAD

1 cup corkscrew macaroni (3 ounces)

1½ cups sliced broccoli flowerets

½ cup pitted ripe olives, halved (optional)

¼ cup sliced green onion (4 medium)

1 cup snipped fresh basil

⅓ cup red wine vinegar

2 tablespoons chopped walnuts or almonds

2 tablespoons grated Parmesan cheese

2 cloves garlic, quartered

⅓ cup olive oil or salad oil

Lettuce leaves

½ cup chopped tomato (1 medium)

Cook pasta according to package directions. Drain pasta. Rinse with *cold* water; drain again.

In a large mixing bowl combine pasta, broccoli, olives (if desired), and green onion.

For pesto, in a blender container or a food processor bowl combine basil, vinegar, nuts, Parmesan cheese, and garlic. Cover and blend or process till smooth. With the machine running, gradually add oil and blend or process till mixture thickens slightly. Pour *half* of the pesto over the pasta mixture. Toss lightly to coat. Cover and chill for 4 to 24 hours. Store remaining pesto for another use (see tip, left).

To serve, line a salad bowl with lettuce leaves. Transfer pasta mixture to the lettuce-lined bowl. Sprinkle with chopped tomato. Makes 6 servings.

PASTA AND BEAN SALAD

For a different look, try wagon wheel macaroni or medium shell macaroni in this pasta salad.

1 cup elbow macaroni (4 ounces)

1 8-ounce can red kidney beans, rinsed and drained

1 cup shredded cheddar cheese **or** Monterey Jack cheese (4 ounces)

½ cup thinly sliced celery (1 stalk)

1 4-ounce can diced green chili peppers

2 tablespoons finely chopped onion

¼ cup mayonnaise **or** salad dressing

¼ cup dairy sour cream

2 tablespoons milk

1 tablespoon snipped fresh oregano **or** 1 teaspoon dried oregano, crushed

Cook pasta according to package directions. Drain pasta. Rinse with *cold* water; drain again.

In a large mixing bowl combine pasta, kidney beans, cheese, celery, chili peppers, and onion.

For dressing, in a small mixing bowl stir together mayonnaise or salad dressing, sour cream, milk, and oregano. Pour dressing over pasta mixture. Toss lightly to coat. Cover and chill for 4 to 24 hours. Before serving, if necessary, stir in additional milk to moisten. Makes 6 servings.

Time

Start to finish	25 min.
Chilling	4 to 24 hrs.

Per Serving

Calories	271
Protein	10 g
Carbohydrate	22 g
Total Fat	16 g
Saturated Fat	6 g
Cholesterol	30 mg
Sodium	426 mg
Potassium	204 mg

GREEK-STYLE PASTA SALAD

Try this new twist on a 24-hour salad—use pasta in place of lettuce. Then slather a creamy garlic dressing atop the layers of pasta, vegetables, and feta cheese.

2 cups cavatelli **or** *elbow macaroni*
Creamy Garlic Dressing (see recipe, page 206)
1 small cucumber, halved and thinly sliced (1¼ cups)
½ cup sliced pitted ripe olives
1 cup crumbled feta cheese (4 ounces)
12 cherry tomatoes, quartered, **or** *1 cup chopped tomato (1 large)*
1 cup alfalfa sprouts
½ cup croutons

Cook pasta according to package directions. Drain pasta. Rinse with *cold* water; drain again.

＊

In a medium mixing bowl combine the pasta and *½ cup* of the Creamy Garlic Dressing. Place the pasta in the bottom of a 2-quart straight-sided glass salad bowl. Layer in the following order: sliced cucumber, olives, cheese, and tomatoes. Spread the remaining Creamy Garlic Dressing evenly over the top of the salad. Top with alfalfa sprouts. Cover tightly with plastic wrap. Chill for 4 to 24 hours. Before serving, sprinkle with croutons. Makes 6 servings.

Time

Start to finish	*30 min.*
Chilling	*4 to 24 hrs.*

Per Serving

Calories	*407*
Protein	*8 g*
Carbohydrate	*28 g*
Total Fat	*30 g*
Saturated Fat	*8 g*
Cholesterol	*37 mg*
Sodium	*542 mg*
Potassium	*151 mg*

Cooking Pasta

If the dried pasta you purchase for a salad doesn't include cooking directions, here's our sure-fire method for cooking it perfectly: In a large saucepan or Dutch oven bring water (about 3 quarts of water for 4 to 8 ounces of pasta) to boiling. If desired, add 1 teaspoon salt and 1 tablespoon olive oil or cooking oil to help keep the pasta separated. Add pasta a little at a time so the water doesn't stop boiling. Reduce heat slightly. Boil, uncovered, for the time specified below or till the pasta is al dente (tender but slightly firm). Stir occasionally. Immediately drain in a colander.

Cavatelli..........................12 minutes

Corkscrew macaroni..................8 to 10 minutes

Elbow macaroni.....................10 minutes

Medium shell macaroni..............8 to 9 minutes

Tortellini.........................15 minutes

Wagon wheel macaroni...............12 minutes

SPINACH AND PASTA SALAD

1½ cups spinach corkscrew macaroni **or** *tricolor corkscrew macaroni (4 ounces)*

1 medium sweet red, yellow, **or** *green pepper, cut into bite-size pieces (1 cup)*

½ cup chopped onion (1 medium)

½ cup cubed cheddar cheese (2 ounces)

2 tablespoons salad oil

2 tablespoons white wine vinegar **or** *white vinegar*

1 teaspoon snipped fresh oregano **or** *¼ teaspoon dried oregano, crushed*

1 teaspoon snipped fresh basil **or** *¼ teaspoon dried basil, crushed*

½ teaspoon pepper

2 cups torn spinach

Cook pasta according to package directions. Drain pasta. Rinse with *cold* water; drain again.

In a large mixing bowl combine pasta, sweet pepper, onion, and cheese.

For dressing, in a screw-top jar combine oil, vinegar, oregano, basil, and pepper. Cover and shake well. Pour dressing over pasta mixture. Toss lightly to coat. Cover and chill for 4 to 24 hours. To serve, toss spinach with pasta mixture. Makes 4 or 5 servings.

When you're shopping for fresh sweet peppers, look for those with the brightest color. Steer away from peppers that are shriveled, bruised, or broken. Cover and refrigerate the peppers and they'll stay fresh for up to 5 days.

Time

Preparation	*25 min.*
Chilling	*4 to 24 hrs.*

Per Serving

Calories	*243*
Protein	*9 g*
Carbohydrate	*26 g*
Total Fat	*12 g*
Saturated Fat	*4 g*
Cholesterol	*15 mg*
Sodium	*124 mg*
Potassium	*353 mg*

If you love creamy macaroni salad, but want something a bit more stylish, give this salad a try.

BASIL TORTELLINI SALAD

1 7-ounce package frozen cheese tortellini or 3½-ounces (2 cups) packaged cheese tortellini

1 small sweet red pepper, cut into bite-size strips

1 cup broccoli flowerets

¾ cup thinly sliced carrot (1 large)

½ cup mayonnaise or salad dressing

2 tablespoons grated Parmesan cheese

1 tablespoon snipped fresh basil or ½ teaspoon dried basil, crushed

1 tablespoon milk

¼ teaspoon pepper

1 clove garlic, minced

¼ cup pine nuts or chopped walnuts

Time

Preparation	30 min.
Chilling	4 to 24 hrs.

Per Serving

Calories	292
Protein	9 g
Carbohydrate	21 g
Total Fat	20 g
Saturated Fat	3 g
Cholesterol	33 mg
Sodium	303 mg
Potassium	231 mg

Cook pasta according to package directions. Drain pasta. Rinse with *cold* water; drain again.

In a large mixing bowl combine pasta, sweet red pepper strips, broccoli flowerets, and sliced carrot.

For dressing, in a small mixing bowl stir together mayonnaise or salad dressing, Parmesan cheese, basil, milk, pepper, and garlic. Pour the dressing over the pasta mixture. Toss lightly to coat. Cover and chill for 4 to 24 hours. Before serving, stir in nuts and, if necessary, additional milk to moisten. Makes 6 servings.

Curried Couscous Salad

⅔ cup water

1 teaspoon instant chicken bouillon granules

⅓ cup couscous

3 tablespoons salad oil

3 tablespoons orange juice

2 tablespoons snipped chutney

1 teaspoon curry powder

⅛ teaspoon dry mustard

⅛ teaspoon ground ginger

⅛ teaspoon ground cinnamon

1 small zucchini, halved lengthwise and thinly sliced (1 cup)

½ cup shredded carrot **or** snipped dried apricots

⅓ cup raisins

2 tablespoons sliced green onion (2 medium)

¼ cup slivered almonds, toasted

In a small saucepan combine water and bouillon granules. Bring to boiling. Remove from heat and stir in couscous. Let stand, covered, for 5 minutes or till liquid is absorbed.

❧

Meanwhile, for dressing, in a screw top jar combine salad oil, orange juice, chutney, curry powder, dry mustard, ginger, and cinnamon. Cover and shake well. Set dressing aside.

❧

In a large mixing bowl combine couscous, zucchini, carrot or apricots, raisins, and green onion. Shake dressing well; pour over salad mixture. Toss lightly to coat. Cover and chill for 4 to 24 hours. Before serving, stir in toasted almonds. Makes 4 servings.

Couscous, made from ground semolina flour and water, is a North African favorite. The tiny, hard pieces get soft and fluffy when they're added to boiling water. Couscous is delicious in this salad of chutney, curry powder, raisins, and almonds.

Time

Preparation	20 min.
Chilling	4 to 24 hrs.

Per Serving

Calories	277
Protein	5 g
Carbohydrate	34 g
Total Fat	15 g
Saturated Fat	2 g
Cholesterol	0 mg
Sodium	318 mg
Potassium	331 mg

Crushed red pepper gives this salad a lot of punch. Plan to serve it with a not-so-peppy main dish such as grilled burgers or broiled chicken.

Time

Preparation	30 min.
Chilling	4 to 24 hrs.

Per Serving

Calories	197
Protein	3 g
Carbohydrate	24 g
Total Fat	11 g
Saturated Fat	1 g
Cholesterol	0 mg
Sodium	213 mg
Potassium	103 mg

RED-PEPPER TWO-GRAIN SALAD

2 cups water

½ cup bulgur

½ cup couscous

1 2¼-ounce can (⅔ cup) sliced pitted ripe olives

½ cup shredded carrot (1 medium)

¼ cup sliced green onion (4 medium)

¼ cup olive oil or salad oil

½ teaspoon finely shredded lime peel

¼ cup lime juice

2 teaspoons sugar

½ to 1 teaspoon crushed red pepper

¼ teaspoon salt

Radicchio leaves

White salad savoy leaves

In a medium saucepan combine water and bulgur. Bring to boiling; reduce heat. Cover and simmer for 10 to 15 minutes or till bulgur is almost tender. Remove from heat; stir in the couscous. Let grain mixture stand, covered, for 5 minutes. Drain mixture. Rinse with cold water. Drain again.

꙰

In a mixing bowl combine the cooked grain mixture, olives, shredded carrot, and sliced green onion; set salad mixture aside.

꙰

For dressing, in a screw-top jar combine olive oil or salad oil, lime peel, lime juice, sugar, red pepper, and salt. Cover and shake well. Pour dressing over salad mixture. Toss lightly to coat. Cover and chill for 4 to 24 hours.

꙰

To serve, line salad plates with radicchio and white salad savoy leaves. Divide salad mixture among plates. Garnish each serving with julienne strips of carrot and a green onion curl, if desired. Makes 6 to 8 servings.

Watching your fat intake? This rice salad would be a good dish in which to try one of the low-fat cheeses that are available.

YELLOW RICE AND AVOCADO SALAD

½ cup long grain rice

½ teaspoon salt

⅛ teaspoon ground saffron **or** *ground turmeric*

Lemon Dressing

3 cups torn romaine

3 cups torn red-tip leaf lettuce

4 slices Swiss cheese, cut into julienne strips (2 ounces)

1 large avocado, seeded, peeled, and sliced

1 medium tomato, thinly sliced

2 hard-cooked eggs, sliced

Cook rice according to package dirctions, *except* add salt and saffron or turmeric. Cool rice slightly. Combine rice and *2 tablespoons* of the Lemon Dressing. Cover and chill for 2 to 24 hours. Cover and chill remaining dressing for 2 to 24 hours.

❧

To serve, in a large salad bowl combine torn romaine and lettuce. Mound rice in the center. Arrange cheese, avocado, tomato, and egg slices around rice. Shake dressing well; pour over salad. Toss lightly to coat. Makes 6 to 8 servings.

LEMON DRESSING

In a screw-top jar combine ¼ cup *olive oil or salad oil,* ¼ cup *water,* 3 tablespoons *lemon juice,* 1 tablespoon *Dijon-style mustard,* 1 teaspoon *sugar,* ½ teaspoon *salt,* and ⅛ teaspoon *pepper.* Cover and shake well.

Time

Preparation	30 min.
Chilling	2 to 24 hrs.

Per Serving

Calories	283
Protein	8 g
Carbohydrate	20 g
Total Fat	20 g
Saturated Fat	4 g
Cholesterol	79 mg
Sodium	490 mg
Potassium	471 mg

Brown Rice and Vegetable Salad

1½ cups cooked brown rice

1¼ cups coarsely chopped, seeded tomato (1 large)

2 medium carrots, cut into julienne strips (1 cup)

½ cup frozen peas

¼ cup sliced green onion (4 medium)

1 tablespoon snipped parsley

1 tablespoon snipped fresh dill or *basil* or *1 teaspoon dried dillweed* or *basil, crushed*

Summer Vinaigrette

Lettuce leaves

In a large mixing bowl stir together cooked rice, chopped tomatoes, carrot strips, peas, green onion, parsley, and dill or basil. Pour Summer Vinaigrette over the rice mixture. Toss lightly to coat. Cover and chill for 4 to 24 hours.

❧

To serve, line a salad bowl with lettuce leaves. Transfer salad to the lettuce-lined bowl. Makes 6 servings.

Summer Vinaigrette

In a screw-top jar combine 3 tablespoons *olive oil or salad oil,* 3 tablespoons *red wine vinegar,* 2 teaspoons *Dijon-style mustard,* 1½ teaspoons *sugar,* and ⅛ teaspoon *pepper.* Cover the jar and shake well.

If you like the texture and the slightly nutty flavor brown rice adds to this salad, consider substituting it for white rice in other salads. Expect some differences, however—brown rice will be chewier and will take longer to cook.

Time

Preparation	50 min.
Chilling	4 to 24 hrs.

Per Serving

Calories	148
Protein	3 g
Carbohydrate	19 g
Total Fat	8 g
Saturated Fat	1 g
Cholesterol	0 mg
Sodium	82 mg
Potassium	195 mg

Apples add color and juicy crispness to this potato salad that's dressed with tangy blue cheese.

APPLE-POTATO SALAD WITH BLUE CHEESE

3 medium potatoes (1 pound)

½ cup mayonnaise or salad dressing

½ cup dairy sour cream

2 tablespoons crumbled blue cheese

1 tablespoon snipped fresh basil or ½ teaspoon dried basil, crushed

¼ teaspoon salt

⅛ teaspoon pepper

1 cup coarsely chopped apple (1 medium)

½ cup thinly sliced celery (1 stalk)

Lettuce leaves

¼ cup coarsely chopped walnuts (optional)

Time

Preparation	35 min.
Chilling	6 to 24 hrs.

Per Serving

Calories	389
Protein	4 g
Carbohydrate	30 g
Total Fat	29 g
Saturated Fat	9 g
Cholesterol	32 mg
Sodium	372 mg
Potassium	571 mg

In a covered saucepan cook potatoes in boiling water for 12 to 15 minutes or till just tender; drain well. Cool slightly. Peel and cube potatoes.

❧

For dressing, in a small mixing bowl combine mayonnaise or salad dressing, sour cream, blue cheese, basil, salt, and pepper. In a large mixing bowl combine dressing, chopped apple, and celery. Add potatoes. Toss lightly to coat. Cover and chill for 6 to 24 hours.

❧

To serve, line a salad bowl with lettuce leaves. Transfer potato salad to the lettuce-lined bowl. If desired, sprinkle with walnuts. Makes 4 to 6 servings.

Artichoke-Potato Salad

If your salad looks a little dry after it's been chilled, stir in an additional 1 to 2 tablespoons of buttermilk or milk.

4 medium potatoes (about 1¼ pounds)

1 9-ounce package frozen cut green beans

1 6½-ounce jar marinated artichoke hearts, drained

Buttermilk-Herb Dressing (see recipe, page 207)

*1 cup red **and/or** yellow baby pear tomatoes **or** cherry tomatoes, halved*

In a covered saucepan cook potatoes in boiling water for 12 to 15 minutes or till just tender; drain well. Cool slightly. Cut potatoes into ¼-inch-thick slices. Meanwhile, cook green beans according to package directions; drain.

In a large mixing bowl place potatoes and green beans. Cut large artichoke hearts in half; add to mixing bowl.

Pour Buttermilk-Herb Dressing over potato mixture. Toss lightly to coat. Cover and chill for 6 to 24 hours. Before serving, stir in tomatoes. Makes 4 to 6 servings.

One Potato, Two Potato, Which Potato?

Confused as to which sack of spuds to pick up at the store when you're going to make potato salad? For salads (and other recipes where you want the potatoes to hold their shape), choose a thin-skinned potato such as round whites or round reds. Their firm and waxy texture keeps them from falling apart when boiled. Mealy-textured, dry, thick-skinned potatoes, such as russets, are better suited for baking and frying.

Time

Preparation	*35 min.*
Chilling	*6 to 24 hrs.*

Per Serving

Calories	*440*
Protein	*7 g*
Carbohydrate	*45 g*
Total Fat	*28 g*
Saturated Fat	*6 g*
Cholesterol	*23 mg*
Sodium	*382 mg*
Potassium	*924 mg*

New potatoes, tomatoes, yellow summer squash, and a walnut vinaigrette make this potato salad extraordinary.

WARM POTATO SALAD WITH WALNUT VINAIGRETTE

¾ pound whole tiny new potatoes, quartered

1 cup cherry tomatoes, halved

1 small yellow summer squash, cut into bite-size strips (1 cup)

½ cup broken walnuts

¼ cup sliced green onion (4 medium)

2 tablespoons snipped fresh tarragon **or** *1 teaspoon dried tarragon, crushed*

Walnut Vinaigrette (see recipe, page 209)

4 cups shredded romaine

Chives (optional)

Chive blossoms (optional)

Time

Start to finish   30 min.

In a covered saucepan cook potatoes in boiling salted water for 12 to 15 minutes or till just tender; drain well.

❦

In a large mixing bowl combine potatoes, tomatoes, yellow summer squash, walnuts, green onion, and tarragon. Pour ⅓ *cup* of the Walnut Vinaigrette over the potato mixture. Toss lightly to coat. Serve immediately on shredded romaine. Garnish with chives and chive blossoms, if desired. Makes 4 servings.

Per Serving

Calories	*467*
Protein	*6 g*
Carbohydrate	*33 g*
Total Fat	*38 g*
Saturated Fat	*3 g*
Cholesterol	*0 mg*
Sodium	*138 mg*
Potassium	*709 mg*

This German-style potato salad lives up to the German culinary tradition of robust and zesty flavors.

HOT HASH BROWN POTATO AND POLISH SAUSAGE SALAD

6 ounces smoked Polish sausage, cut into ¼-inch-thick slices

1 tablespoon cooking oil

1 clove garlic, minced

1 small green pepper, cut into bite-size strips (¾ cup)

½ cup chopped onion (1 medium)

1 tablespoon all-purpose flour

1 tablespoon sugar

1 tablespoon coarse-grain brown mustard

⅛ to ¼ teaspoon pepper

½ cup chicken broth or water

¼ cup vinegar

1 12-ounce package loose-pack frozen hash brown potatoes, thawed

Time

Start to finish   25 min.

Per Serving

Calories	396
Protein	10 g
Carbohydrate	34 g
Total Fat	26 g
Saturated Fat	9 g
Cholesterol	30 mg
Sodium	547 mg
Potassium	581 mg

In a large skillet cook Polish sausage in hot oil for 2 to 3 minutes or till lightly browned. Remove sausage from skillet, reserving drippings in skillet. Drain sausage on paper towels.

❧

For dressing, cook garlic, green pepper, and onion in reserved drippings till tender but not brown. Stir in flour, sugar, mustard, and pepper. Stir in chicken broth or water and vinegar. Cook and stir till thickened and bubbly. Stir in thawed potatoes and Polish sausage. Cook for 4 to 5 minutes or till potatoes are tender, stirring gently. Serve immediately. Makes 4 servings.

CHILI PEPPER POTATO SALAD

1 pound whole tiny new potatoes, cut into ¼-inch-thick slices

¼ cup bottled creamy cucumber salad dressing **or** *bottled creamy bacon salad dressing*

1 4-ounce can diced green chili peppers, drained

⅛ teaspoon pepper

1 clove garlic, minced

1 cup frozen peas

½ cup coarsely chopped sweet yellow **and/or** *red pepper (1 small)*

In a covered saucepan cook potatoes in boiling salted water for 12 to 15 minutes or till tender; drain well. Cool potatoes slightly.

❧

Meanwhile, for dressing, in a small mixing bowl stir together creamy cucumber or creamy bacon salad dressing, green chili peppers, pepper, and garlic.

❧

In a large mixing bowl combine dressing, peas, and sweet yellow or red peppers. Add potatoes. Toss lightly to coat. Cover and chill for 6 to 24 hours. Makes 4 to 6 servings.

Counting calories? Use a reduced-calorie ranch-style salad dressing on this unusual potato combo.

Time

Preparation	30 min.
Chilling	6 to 24 hrs.

Per Serving

Calories	238
Protein	5 g
Carbohydrate	36 g
Total Fat	9 g
Saturated Fat	0 g
Cholesterol	0 mg
Sodium	467 mg
Potassium	639 mg

MOLDED POTATO SALAD

For your next picnic, prepare this refreshing slice-and-serve potato salad.

2 medium potatoes (about 6 ounces each), peeled and cut into ½-inch cubes

⅓ cup finely chopped celery

¼ cup sliced green onion (4 medium)

2 tablespoons sweet pickle relish

1 tablespoon snipped fresh dill or 1 teaspoon dried dillweed

⅛ teaspoon white pepper

1½ cups chicken broth

1 envelope unflavored gelatin

3 tablespoons white wine vinegar or white vinegar

½ cup mayonnaise or salad dressing

2 teaspoons prepared mustard

2 hard-cooked eggs, chopped

Lettuce leaves

Time

Preparation	*1¼ hrs.*
Chilling	*6 hrs.*

Per Serving

Calories	*193*
Protein	*6 g*
Carbohydrate	*15 g*
Total Fat	*13 g*
Saturated Fat	*3 g*
Cholesterol	*61 mg*
Sodium	*296 mg*
Potassium	*358 mg*

In a covered saucepan cook potatoes in boiling water for 12 to 15 minutes or till just tender; drain well.

In a medium mixing bowl combine potatoes, celery, green onion, pickle relish, dill, and white pepper. Toss lightly to mix; set aside.

In a small saucepan combine *1 cup* of the chicken broth and the gelatin. Let stand 5 minutes to soften. Cook and stir over medium heat till gelatin is dissolved; pour into a large mixing bowl. Stir in remaining chicken broth and vinegar. Chill (see tip, page 183) till partially set (the consistency of unbeaten egg whites).

Add mayonnaise or salad dressing and mustard to partially set gelatin. Beat with a rotary beater till mixed. Fold the potato mixture and hard-cooked eggs into the gelatin mixture. Spoon into a lightly oiled 5-cup ring mold. Chill for at least 6 hours or till firm.

To serve, line a serving platter with lettuce leaves. Dip mold into warm water for a few seconds to loosen edges. Unmold salad (see tip, page 185) onto the lettuce-lined platter. If desired, garnish with additional fresh dill and sliced hard-cooked egg. Makes 8 servings.

CREAMY BROCCOLI MOLD

For lemon peel strips, use a vegetable peeler to cut the peel off a lemon. With a sharp knife, cut the peel into fine strips. If desired, tie the strips into bows or knots.

2 cups coarsely chopped broccoli flowerets and stems (about ½ pound)
or one 10-ounce package frozen chopped broccoli

½ cup whipping cream

1 teaspoon finely shredded lemon peel

4 teaspoons lemon juice

1 teaspoon snipped fresh basil or ¼ teaspoon dried basil, crushed

¼ teaspoon white pepper

1 cup chicken broth

1 envelope unflavored gelatin

Lettuce leaves

Lemon peel strips (optional)

In a covered medium saucepan cook fresh broccoli in a small amount of boiling water for 5 to 7 minutes or till tender. (Cook frozen broccoli according to package directions.) Drain well. In a blender container or food processor bowl combine cooked broccoli, whipping cream, shredded lemon peel, lemon juice, basil, and white pepper. Cover and blend or process just till smooth. Transfer mixture to a medium mixing bowl; set aside.

※

In a small saucepan combine chicken broth and gelatin. Let stand 5 minutes to soften. Cook and stir over medium heat till gelatin is dissolved. Stir gelatin mixture into the broccoli mixture. Pour into 4 lightly oiled individual molds or one lightly oiled 3½-cup mold. Chill for at least 6 hours or till firm.

※

To serve, dip each mold into warm water for a few seconds to loosen edges. Unmold salads (see tip, page 185) onto 4 lettuce-lined salad plates. (For the large mold, unmold the salad onto a lettuce-lined serving platter.) If desired, garnish with lemon peel strips. Makes 4 servings.

Time

Preparation	30 min.
Chilling	6 hrs.

Per Serving

Calories	135
Protein	5 g
Carbohydrate	5 g
Total Fat	12 g
Saturated Fat	7 g
Cholesterol	41 mg
Sodium	221 mg
Potassium	260 mg

This two-layer salad creation can double as a dessert.

STRAWBERRIES AND CREAM MOLD

1 10-ounce package frozen sliced strawberries, thawed

1 cup apple juice

1 3-ounce package strawberry-flavored gelatin

1 8¼-ounce can crushed pineapple

½ cup water

¼ cup sugar

1 envelope unflavored gelatin

1 8-ounce carton dairy sour cream

¼ cup water

½ teaspoon finely shredded lemon peel

1 tablespoon lemon juice

Lettuce leaves

Time

Preparation	1¼ hrs.
Chilling	6 hrs.

Per Serving

Calories	170
Protein	2 g
Carbohydrate	29 g
Total Fat	6 g
Saturated Fat	4 g
Cholesterol	13 mg
Sodium	25 mg
Potassium	146 mg

Drain the strawberries, reserving juice; set aside. In a medium saucepan bring *¾ cup* of the apple juice to boiling; remove from heat. Add strawberry-flavored gelatin, stirring till dissolved. Stir in remaining apple juice and reserved strawberry juice. Chill (see tip, page 183) till partially set (the consistency of unbeaten egg whites).

⬥

Stir strawberries into partially set gelatin. Pour the strawberry mixture into a 9x9x2-inch baking pan. Chill till almost firm (mixture is sticky to the touch and appears set, but if tipped will flow to one side).

⬥

Meanwhile, drain pineapple, reserving juice; set aside. In a medium saucepan combine the ½ cup water, sugar, and unflavored gelatin. Let stand 5 minutes to soften. Cook and stir over medium heat till gelatin is dissolved. Stir in reserved pineapple juice, sour cream, the ¼ cup water, lemon peel, and lemon juice. Beat with a rotary beater till smooth. Chill till partially set (the consistency of unbeaten egg whites). Stir pineapple into partially set gelatin. Pour over strawberry layer. Chill for at least 6 hours or till firm.

⬥

To serve, line 9 salad plates with lettuce leaves. Cut salad into squares and serve on the lettuce-lined plates. Makes 9 servings.

FROSTY FRUIT SALAD

Use a container of plain soft-style cream cheese and 1 tablespoon of honey if you can't find cream cheese with honey.

1 8-ounce container soft-style cream cheese with honey

1 cup coarsely chopped ripe bananas (2 medium)

¼ cup whipping cream

*1 11-ounce can mandarin orange sections, drained **and** coarsely chopped*

½ cup coarsely chopped, pitted dates

Lettuce leaves

In a small mixing bowl combine cream cheese and chopped bananas. Beat with an electric mixer on medium speed about 30 seconds or till well combined. Gradually add whipping cream, beating till mixed. Stir in chopped mandarin orange sections and dates.

❦

Line 8 muffin cups with paper bake cups. Spoon the fruit mixture into the paper-lined muffin cups. Cover and freeze for at least 4 hours or till firm.

❦

To serve, remove salads from freezer; let stand at room temperature for 30 to 40 minutes or till slightly thawed. Meanwhile, line 8 salad plates with lettuce leaves. Remove the paper bake cups. Serve salads on the lettuce-lined plates. Makes 8 servings.

Time

Preparation	10 min.
Freezing	4 hrs.
Thawing	30 to 40 min.

Per Serving

Calories	204
Protein	3 g
Carbohydrate	22 g
Total Fat	13 g
Saturated Fat	7 g
Cholesterol	40 mg
Sodium	107 mg
Potassium	250 mg

We've scooped this temptingly tart, first-course salad as you would ice cream for an elegant presentation. For a more casual look, see the recipe note below.

CRANBERRY APPETIZER SALAD

2½ cups water

1 12-ounce package cranberries (3 cups)

1½ cups sugar

½ teaspoon unflavored gelatin

¼ cup lemon juice

Fresh mint leaves

Lemon peel strips (optional)

Dianthus or other edible flower (optional)

In a medium saucepan heat water to boiling. Add cranberries; return to boiling. Reduce heat; boil gently over medium-high heat for 3 to 4 minutes or till the cranberry skins pop, stirring occasionally. Remove from heat. Press the mixture through a food mill or sieve to remove skins; discard the skins.

In the same saucepan stir together sugar and gelatin. Stir in the sieved cranberry mixture. Cook and stir over medium heat till sugar dissolves. Remove from heat; stir in lemon juice*.

Transfer the cranberry mixture to an 8x8x2-inch baking pan. Cover and freeze about 4 hours or till nearly firm. Break frozen mixture into small chunks. Transfer to a chilled bowl. Beat with an electric mixer till smooth but not melted. Return to baking pan; cover and freeze about 4 hours or till firm.

To serve, arrange fresh mint leaves on 6 salad plates. Scrape a large spoon across the surface of the frozen salad mixture and mound it onto plates. Garnish with lemon peel strips and dianthus, if desired. Makes 6 servings.

*NOTE: At this point, you can spoon the cranberry mixture into 6 muffin cups lined with paper bake cups and freeze till firm. To serve, peel off the bake cups and place on mint- or lettuce-lined plates.

Time

Preparation	20 min.
Freezing	4 hrs.
Beating	5 min
Freezing	4 hrs.

Per Serving

Calories	219
Protein	0 g
Carbohydrate	57 g
Total Fat	0 g
Saturated Fat	0 g
Cholesterol	0 mg
Sodium	2 mg
Potassium	48 mg

Whether you choose raspberries or blackberries, look for berries that are plump, shiny, and firm.

PINEAPPLE-BERRY FROZEN SALAD

2 8-ounce cartons pineapple yogurt

1 8-ounce container soft-style cream cheese with pineapple

1 4-ounce container frozen whipped dessert topping, thawed

1 8-ounce can crushed pineapple, drained

1 cup fresh **or** *frozen unsweetened red raspberries* **or** *blackberries*

¼ cup chopped pecans, toasted

Lettuce leaves

Time

Preparation	20 min.
Freezing	8 hrs.
Thawing	1 hr.

Per Serving

Calories	216
Protein	4 g
Carbohydrate	22 g
Total Fat	13 g
Saturated Fat	8 g
Cholesterol	25 mg
Sodium	113 mg
Potassium	228 mg

In a medium mixing bowl combine yogurt and cream cheese. Beat with an electric mixer on medium speed till smooth. Stir in whipped topping, pineapple, raspberries or blackberries, and pecans. Pour into an 8x8x2-inch baking pan. Cover and freeze for at least 8 hours or till firm.

To serve, remove salad from the freezer; let stand at room temperature about 1 hour or till slightly thawed. Meanwhile, line salad plates with lettuce leaves. Cut the salad into squares; serve on lettuce-lined plates. Makes 9 to 12 servings.

FRUIT AND WINE MOLD

This sparkling extravaganza features the pick of fresh summer fruits—peaches, strawberries, and grapes.

2 cups water

1 6-ounce package peach-, lemon-, or orange-flavored gelatin

¾ cup dry white wine or white grape juice

1 10-ounce bottle ginger ale

1½ cups cut-up, peeled peaches or 1½ cups frozen peach slices, thawed and cut up

1 cup sliced strawberries

½ cup seedless red or green grapes, halved

In a medium saucepan bring water to boiling; remove from heat. Add peach-, lemon-, or orange-flavored gelatin, stirring till dissolved. Stir in wine or white grape juice. Slowly stir in ginger ale. Chill (see tip, below) till partially set (the consistency of unbeaten egg whites).

❧

Stir peaches, strawberries, and grapes into partially set gelatin. Spoon into a lightly oiled 6½-cup ring mold. Chill for at least 6 hours or till firm.

❧

To serve, dip mold into warm water for a few seconds to loosen edges. Unmold salad (see tip, page 185) onto a serving plate. Makes 8 servings.

Time

Preparation	45 min.
Chilling	6 hrs.

Per Serving

Calories	74
Protein	1 g
Carbohydrate	15 g
Total Fat	0 g
Saturated Fat	0 g
Cholesterol	0 mg
Sodium	18 mg
Potassium	127 mg

Quick Gel

To make preparing gelatin salads less time-consuming, speed up the gelling process. First, fill a large mixing bowl with ice cubes and water. Then, place the saucepan containing the dissolved gelatin mixture in the ice water. Using a spoon, stir the gelatin mixture as it sets up. Gelatin takes about 30 minutes to become partially set using this method. It takes about 1 hour in the refrigerator. We computed our gelatin salad preparation times using this time-saving, ice-water method.

When the temperature soars on summer days, serve this cooling peach and strawberry salad.

FROZEN FRUIT SALAD

1 cup chopped peeled peaches **or** *nectarines*

1 cup chopped strawberries

1 3-ounce package cream cheese, softened

⅓ cup dairy sour cream

¼ cup sugar

¼ cup halved seedless grapes

2 tablespoons chopped almonds, toasted

1 teaspoon finely shredded lemon peel

Leaf lettuce leaves

Place ¼ *cup* of the chopped peaches or nectarines, ¼ *cup* of the chopped strawberries, the cream cheese, sour cream, and sugar in a blender container or food processor bowl. Cover and blend or process till smooth. Transfer the mixture to a mixing bowl.

Stir grapes, almonds, lemon peel, the remaining peaches or nectarines, and the remaining strawberries into the cream cheese mixture. Pour into a 9x5x3-inch loaf pan. Cover and freeze for at least 6 hours or till firm.

To serve, remove salad from the freezer; let stand at room temperature about 30 minutes or till slightly thawed. Meanwhile, line 6 salad plates with lettuce leaves. Cut salad lengthwise in half, then crosswise to make 6 pieces. Makes 6 servings.

Time

Preparation	20 min.
Freezing	6 hrs.
Thawing	30 min.

Per Serving

Calories	152
Protein	3 g
Carbohydrate	16 g
Total Fat	9 g
Saturated Fat	5 g
Cholesterol	21 mg
Sodium	51 mg
Potassium	192 mg

Molded Cranberry Salad

1¼ cups orange juice

1 3-ounce package raspberry- **or** strawberry-flavored gelatin

1 cup cranberry-orange, cranberry-raspberry, **or** cranberry-strawberry sauce

1 cup whipping cream

1 cup chopped pear **or** apple (1 medium)

Lettuce leaves

Orange slices (optional)

In a medium saucepan bring orange juice to boiling; remove from heat. Add gelatin, stirring till dissolved. Stir in cranberry-orange, cranberry-raspberry, or cranberry-strawberry sauce. Chill (see tip, page 183) till partially set (the consistency of unbeaten egg whites).

In a chilled small mixing bowl, beat whipping cream till soft peaks form. Fold whipped cream and chopped pear or apple into partially set gelatin. Chill till mixture mounds when dropped from a spoon. Spoon gelatin mixture into a lightly oiled 4-cup ring mold. Chill for at least 6 hours or till firm.

To serve, dip mold into warm water for a few seconds to loosen edges. Unmold (see tip, below) onto a lettuce-lined serving platter. Garnish with orange slices, if desired. Makes 6 servings.

Unmolding Gelatin Salads

To unmold your gelatin salad with finesse, dip the mold into warm water for a few seconds to loosen the edges from the salad. Then, center a plate upside down over the mold. Hold the mold and plate together and invert them. Shake the mold gently until you feel the salad loosen, then carefully lift the mold off. If the salad doesn't unmold, repeat these steps.

The tangy cranberry sauce used in this recipe comes in three flavor variations. Look for these shelf-stable products, packed in plastic containers, alongside the canned cranberry sauces on your grocer's shelf.

Time

Preparation	45 min.
Chilling	6 hrs.

Per Serving

Calories	274
Protein	2 g
Carbohydrate	35 g
Total Fat	15 g
Saturated Fat	9 g
Cholesterol	54 mg
Sodium	41 mg
Potassium	217 mg

Although the recipe calls for pineapple, oranges, and grapes, you can use any fruit you like, such as plums, peaches, kiwi fruit, or apples.

TROPICAL FRUIT PLATE

1 8¼-ounce can pineapple chunks

½ cup dairy sour cream

¼ cup mayonnaise or salad dressing

½ teaspoon finely shredded lime peel

1 teaspoon lime juice

⅛ teaspoon ground mace or nutmeg

Boston or Bibb lettuce leaves

3 tangelos or 2 oranges

1 cup seedless red grapes, halved

⅓ cup coconut, toasted

Lime slices (optional)

Time

Start to finish   20 min.

Per Serving

Calories	196
Protein	2 g
Carbohydrate	21 g
Total Fat	13 g
Saturated Fat	5 g
Cholesterol	14 mg
Sodium	65 mg
Potassium	236 mg

Drain pineapple chunks, reserving *1 tablespoon* of the juice. Set pineapple chunks aside.

For dressing, in a small mixing bowl stir together reserved pineapple juice, sour cream, mayonnaise or salad dressing, lime peel, lime juice, and mace or nutmeg. Cover and chill till serving time.

To serve, line 6 salad plates with lettuce leaves. Peel and section tangelos or oranges. Evenly divide pineapple chunks, tangelo or orange sections, and grapes among the lettuce-lined plates. Pour dressing over each salad; sprinkle each with toasted coconut. Garnish with lime slices, if desired. Makes 6 servings.

PEAR SALAD
WITH RASPBERRY VINAIGRETTE

This salad tastes best when the pears are perfectly ripe. Buy pears that are firm, but not hard. Put them in a paper bag for a few days to ripen.

Raspberry Vinaigrette

4 cups torn mixed greens

2 pears, cored and sliced

1 cup seedless red grapes, halved

¼ cup chopped pecans (optional)

Prepare Raspberry Vinaigrette. Cover and chill for at least 1 hour.

❧

Arrange the torn mixed greens on 4 salad plates. Arrange pear slices and grapes on the greens. Sprinkle each plate with pecans, if desired. Stir Raspberry Vinaigrette well; pour over each salad. Makes 4 servings.

RASPBERRY VINAIGRETTE

In a blender container or a food processor bowl combine 1 cup fresh *or* frozen *raspberries* (thaw raspberries, if frozen) and ¼ cup *red wine vinegar*. Cover and blend or process about 30 seconds or till the raspberries are puréed. Sieve the mixture to remove the seeds; discard seeds. Transfer the pureed raspberry mixture to a small mixing bowl. Stir in ¼ cup *salad oil*, 1 to 2 tablespoons *sugar,* and ¼ teaspoon *ground cinnamon.* Cover and chill for at least 1 hour. Makes about ⅔ cup.

Time

Preparation	15 min.
Chilling	1 hr.

Per Serving

Calories	232
Protein	2 g
Carbohydrate	27 g
Total Fat	14 g
Saturated Fat	2 g
Cholesterol	0 mg
Sodium	11 mg
Potassium	352 mg

A taste-bud-tingling orange and poppy seed vinaigrette dresses this refreshing fruit and greens salad.

CITRUS AND PAPAYA SALAD

¼ cup salad oil

1 teaspoon finely shredded orange peel

¼ cup orange juice

1½ teaspoons poppy seed

1 papaya

1 red grapefruit

1 head Belgian endive

Boston **or** *Bibb lettuce leaves*

⅓ cup sliced almonds (optional)

Red-tip Belgian endive leaves (optional)

Time

Preparation	15 min.
Chilling	1 hr.

Per Serving

Calories	189
Protein	2 g
Carbohydrate	16 g
Total Fat	14 g
Saturated Fat	2 g
Cholesterol	0 mg
Sodium	5 mg
Potassium	441 mg

For dressing, in a screw-top jar combine salad oil, orange peel, orange juice, and poppy seed. Cover and shake well. Chill for at least 1 hour.

Seed, peel, and slice papaya lengthwise. Peel and section grapefruit. Slice the Belgian endive crosswise into 8 pieces.

Line 4 salad plates with the Boston or Bibb lettuce leaves. Arrange the papaya slices, grapefruit sections, and sliced Belgian endive atop the lettuce leaves. Sprinkle with almonds, if desired. Shake dressing well; pour over each salad. Garnish each serving with the red-tip Belgian endive leaves, if desired. Makes 4 servings.

Serve this holiday salad as a nifty variation on cranberry-orange relish.

CRANBERRY-ORANGE SALAD

2 cups cranberries

½ cup water

¼ cup sugar

¼ cup white wine vinegar **or** white vinegar

2 tablespoons walnut oil **or** salad oil

2 tablespoons honey

6 cups torn spinach

3 oranges, peeled and thinly sliced

½ pound jicama **or** celeriac, peeled and cut into thin strips (1 cup)

¼ cup broken walnuts, toasted

Time

Preparation	10 min.
Chilling	2 hrs.
Assembling	20 min.

Per Serving

Calories	193
Protein	3 g
Carbohydrate	31 g
Total Fat	8 g
Saturated Fat	1 g
Cholesterol	0 mg
Sodium	50 mg
Potassium	523 mg

In a medium saucepan combine cranberries, water, and sugar. Bring to boiling, stirring to dissolve sugar. Cover and gently boil about 2 minutes or just till cranberry skins pop. Transfer cranberry mixture to a medium mixing bowl. Cover and chill for at least 2 hours.

For dressing, drain cranberries, reserving *1 tablespoon* of the liquid; set cranberries aside. In a screw-top jar combine reserved cranberry liquid, white wine vinegar or white vinegar, walnut oil or salad oil, and honey. Cover and shake well.

Arrange spinach on 6 salad plates. Arrange orange slices and cranberries atop lettuce. Top with jicama or celeriac and sprinkle with walnuts. Shake dressing well; pour over each salad. Makes 6 servings.

MULLED FRUIT BOWL

For an eye-opening brunch dish, mix up this flavorful fruit combination the day before and let it chill overnight.

2 tablespoons aniseed

1 cup water

¾ cup sugar

1 tablespoon lemon juice

½ of a small pineapple (about 1½ pounds) **or** *one 15½-ounce can pineapple chunks, drained*

½ of a small honeydew melon

½ of a small cantaloupe

1 orange, peeled, sliced, and quartered

1 nectarine, cut into thin wedges

1 plum, cut into thin wedges

½ cup seedless red **or** *green grapes*

½ of a lime, sliced

Cabbage leaves **or** *lettuce leaves*

For marinade, place aniseed in the center of an 8-inch square of several layers of 100-percent cotton cheesecloth. Bring edges together; tie with string. In a small saucepan combine the cheesecloth bag, water, sugar, and lemon juice. Bring to boiling, stirring till sugar dissolves. Cook, uncovered, over medium heat for 5 to 7 minutes or till the mixture is golden and the consistency of a thin syrup (you should have about 1 cup syrup). *Do not remove the cheesecloth bag.* Cool syrup slightly.

❧

Meanwhile, peel, core, and cut the pineapple into bite-size pieces. Remove the seeds from the honeydew melon and cantaloupe. Use a melon baller to scoop out the pulp from the honeydew melon and the cantaloupe.

❧

In a 3- to 4-quart mixing bowl combine pineapple, honeydew melon, cantaloupe, orange pieces, nectarine wedges, plum wedges, grapes, and lime slices. Add the syrup; toss lightly to coat fruit. Cover and marinate for 4 to 24 hours, stirring occasionally.

❧

To serve, remove the cheesecloth bag. Line salad plates with cabbage leaves or lettuce leaves. Using a slotted spoon, transfer fruit to salad plates. Makes 10 servings.

Time

Preparation	*25 min.*
Marinating	*4 to 24 hrs.*

Per Serving

Calories	*134*
Protein	*1 g*
Carbohydrate	*34 g*
Total Fat	*1 g*
Saturated Fat	*0 g*
Cholesterol	*0 mg*
Sodium	*8 mg*
Potassium	*362 mg*

Fresh mint, honey, and orange peel perk up this fresh-tasting fruit cup.

HONEY, PRUNE, AND CITRUS SALAD

2 medium oranges

2 medium grapefruit

Orange juice

8 pitted prunes, cut in half

1 tablespoon snipped fresh mint **or** *½ teaspoon dried mint, crushed*

1 tablespoon honey

Lettuce leaves

Fresh mint (optional)

Time

Preparation	20 min.
Chilling	2 to 24 hrs.

Per Serving

Calories	132
Protein	2 g
Carbohydrate	34 g
Total Fat	0 g
Saturated Fat	0 g
Cholesterol	0 mg
Sodium	3 mg
Potassium	475 mg

Finely shred enough orange peel from 1 of the oranges to equal 1 teaspoon; set orange peel aside. Working over a mixing bowl to catch the juices, peel and section the oranges and the grapefruit. Set aside orange and grapefruit sections. Transfer the juice mixture to a measuring cup. Add enough additional orange juice to equal ⅓ cup.

In a small saucepan combine the juice mixture and the prunes. Bring to boiling; remove from heat. Stir in the orange peel, mint, and honey. Transfer mixture to a mixing bowl. Gently stir in the orange and grapefruit sections. Cover and chill for 2 to 24 hours.

To serve, line 4 salad bowls with lettuce leaves. Using a slotted spoon, transfer the fruit mixture to the lettuce-lined bowls. Garnish each salad bowl with fresh mint, if desired. Makes 4 servings.

SUMMER FRUIT SALAD

Instead of cantaloupe shells, you can serve the fruit in sherbet dishes or on lettuce-lined plates.

2 medium cantaloupes

*2 cups sliced, peeled peaches **or** sliced nectarines (2 medium)*

*2 cups blueberries **and/or** halved strawberries*

2 tablespoons peach liqueur

2 tablespoons honey

1 tablespoon lemon juice

⅛ teaspoon ground cinnamon

Fresh mint (optional)

Cut each cantaloupe lengthwise in half. Remove the seeds. Use a melon baller to scoop out the pulp. Chill *2 cups* of the melon balls till serving time (chill the remaining melon balls for another use).

⋇

If desired, lay the melon shells on their sides. Using the melon baller, press down onto the edges of the shells, cutting scalloped edges. Trim a thin slice from the bottom of each melon shell. Place each shell on a salad plate; set aside.

⋇

In a large mixing bowl combine the 2 cups of melon balls, the peaches or nectarines, and the blueberries or strawberries.

⋇

For dressing, in a small mixing bowl combine peach liqueur, honey, lemon juice, and cinnamon. Pour over fruit mixture. Toss lightly to coat. Spoon the fruit mixture into the melon shells. Garnish each salad with fresh mint, if desired. Makes 4 servings.

Time

Start to finish   25 min.

Per Serving

Calories	218
Protein	3 g
Carbohydrate	50 g
Total Fat	1 g
Saturated Fat	0 g
Cholesterol	0 mg
Sodium	27 mg
Potassium	1,133 mg

Drizzle this tasty mint and raspberry dressing over any combination of fresh fruit.

Time

Start to finish   15 min.

Per Serving

Calories	216
Protein	2 g
Carbohydrate	23 g
Total Fat	15 g
Saturated Fat	2 g
Cholesterol	0 mg
Sodium	8 mg
Potassium	560 mg

GRAPEFRUIT AND AVOCADO SALAD

2 tablespoons salad oil

2 tablespoons raspberry vinegar

1 teaspoon sugar

½ teaspoon snipped fresh mint **or** *pinch dried mint, crushed*

Boston, Bibb, **or** *leaf lettuce leaves*

2 medium red grapefruit, peeled and sectioned

1 medium avocado, seeded, peeled, and sliced

1 medium pear, cored and sliced

½ cup raspberries **or** *¼ cup pomegranate seeds*

For dressing, in a screw-top jar combine salad oil, raspberry vinegar, sugar, and mint. Cover and shake well.

Line 4 salad plates with lettuce leaves. On each plate arrange grapefruit sections, avocado slices, and pear slices. Top each serving with raspberries or pomegranate seeds. Shake dressing well; pour over each salad. Makes 4 servings.

APPLE COLESLAW

Chopped apple and vanilla yogurt sweeten this variation of a classic coleslaw.

*¼ cup mayonnaise **or** salad dressing*

¼ cup vanilla yogurt

1 tablespoon milk

⅛ teaspoon salt

⅛ teaspoon ground cinnamon

2½ cups shredded cabbage (½ of a small head)

1 cup chopped apple (1 medium)

½ cup shredded carrot (1 medium)

3 tablespoons sliced green onion (3 medium)

For dressing, in a small mixing bowl stir together mayonniase or salad dressing, vanilla yogurt, milk, salt, and cinnamon.

❦

In a large mixing bowl combine shredded cabbage, chopped apple, shredded carrot, and sliced green onion. Pour the dressing over the cabbage mixture. Toss lightly to coat. Cover and chill for 2 to 24 hours. Makes 6 servings.

Time

Preparation	20 min.
Chilling	2 to 24 hrs.

Per Serving

Calories	66
Protein	1 g
Carbohydrate	8 g
Total Fat	4 g
Saturated Fat	1 g
Cholesterol	4 mg
Sodium	123 mg
Potassium	153 mg

195

To keep the Oriental noodles crisp and crunchy, we've added them to the salad just before serving.

ORIENTAL CABBAGE SALAD

1 3-ounce package Oriental noodles with chicken flavor

¼ cup salad oil

*¼ cup rice vinegar **or** white wine vinegar*

1 tablespoon sugar

¼ teaspoon pepper

1 8¾-ounce can baby corn, drained

*2 cups shredded red **and/or** green cabbage*

*1 cup fresh pea pods **or** ½ of a 6-ounce package frozen pea pods*

1 7-ounce jar whole straw mushrooms, drained

¼ cup sliced green onion (4 medium)

Chinese cabbage leaves

2 teaspoons sesame seed, toasted (optional)

4 radishes, halved lengthwise (optional)

Time

Preparation	*15 min.*
Chilling	*4 to 24 hrs.*

Per Serving

Calories	*208*
Protein	*5 g*
Carbohydrate	*17 g*
Total Fat	*15 g*
Saturated Fat	*2 g*
Cholesterol	*0 mg*
Sodium	*259 mg*
Potassium	*250 mg*

For dressing, in a screw-top jar combine the seasoning package from the Oriental noodles, salad oil, vinegar, sugar, and pepper. Cover and shake well to dissolve seasonings.

Cut each ear of baby corn crosswise in half. In a large mixing bowl combine baby corn, cabbage, pea pods, straw mushrooms, and green onion. Shake dressing well; pour over cabbage mixture. Toss lightly to coat. Cover and chill for 4 to 24 hours.

To serve, break dry Oriental noodles into pieces. Add noodles to cabbage mixture; toss lightly to mix. Line 4 salad plates with cabbage leaves. Divide cabbage mixture among the cabbage-lined plates. If desired, sprinkle each serving with toasted sesame seed and garnish with radishes. Makes 4 servings.

This creamy vege-table toss makes a light alternative to potato salad.

VEGETABLE SALAD WITH BUTTERMILK-HERB DRESSING

2 cups cauliflower flowerets **and/or** *broccoli flowerets*

1 small yellow summer squash **or** *zucchini, halved lengthwise and thinly sliced (1½ cups)*

1 large sweet red, yellow, **or** *green pepper, cut into bite-size strips*

1 cup sliced radishes

1 cup frozen peas

3 tablespoons thinly sliced green onion (3 medium)

½ cup Buttermilk-Herb Dressing (see recipe, page 207)

In a large mixing bowl combine cauliflower or broccoli flowerets, summer squash or zucchini, sweet pepper strips, radishes, peas, and green onion. Pour Buttermilk-Herb Dressing over vegetables. Toss lightly to coat. Cover and chill for 4 to 12 hours. Makes 4 to 6 servings.

Think Fresh

Superb salads start with garden-fresh vegetables and perfectly ripe fruits. Unless you have a garden in your own backyard, there's nothing fresher than produce from a local farmers' market. Most cities and towns hold farmers' markets at least weekly through the summer months. Check your newspaper or call the chamber of commerce to see on what day of the week the farmers' market falls in your community.

Time

Preparation	20 min.
Chilling	4 to 12 hrs.

Per Serving

Calories	178
Protein	4 g
Carbohydrate	14 g
Total Fat	13 g
Saturated Fat	3 g
Cholesterol	12 mg
Sodium	143 mg
Potassium	490 mg

DIJON ASPARAGUS SALAD

Asparagus and bow tie macaroni make this pasta salad an elegant creation.

4 ounces medium bow tie macaroni

1¾ cups asparagus cut diagonally into 1½-inch pieces (about ½ pound)

¼ cup finely chopped onion (½ of a medium)

⅓ cup mayonnaise or salad dressing

2 tablespoons Dijon-style mustard

1 to 2 tablespoons milk (optional)

8 cherry tomatoes, quartered

Coarsely ground pepper

In a large saucepan cook pasta in boiling water for 5 minutes. Add asparagus and cook for 3 to 4 minutes more or till pasta is tender but still slightly firm and asparagus is crisp-tender. Drain pasta and asparagus. Rinse with *cold* water; drain again. Transfer pasta and asparagus to a large mixing bowl; add chopped onion.

❧

For dressing, in a small mixing bowl stir together mayonnaise or salad dressing and mustard. Pour dressing over pasta mixture. Toss lightly to coat. Cover and chill for 4 to 24 hours.

❧

Before serving, if necessary, stir in milk to moisten. Add cherry tomatoes; toss lightly to mix. Sprinkle with pepper. Makes 6 servings.

Time

Preparation	25 min.
Chilling	4 to 24 hrs.

Per Serving

Calories	180
Protein	5 g
Carbohydrate	20 g
Total Fat	11 g
Saturated Fat	2 g
Cholesterol	7 mg
Sodium	227 mg
Potassium	175 mg

If you have a vegetable garden, pluck a zucchini blossom to garnish this sautéed vegetable salad.

Time

Preparation	20 min.
Chilling	4 to 24 hrs.

Per Serving

Calories	103
Protein	2 g
Carbohydrate	8 g
Total Fat	8 g
Saturated Fat	1 g
Cholesterol	0 mg
Sodium	227 mg
Potassium	333 mg

RATATOUILLE-STYLE SALAD

2 small zucchini, halved lengthwise and cut into ½-inch-thick pieces (2 cups)

½ cup chopped onion (1 medium)

¼ cup chopped sweet yellow pepper (½ of a small)

¼ cup chopped sweet red pepper (½ of a small)

2 tablespoons olive oil or salad oil

1 cup chopped tomato (1 large)

⅓ cup sliced pitted ripe olives

4 teaspoons snipped fresh basil or 1¼ teaspoons dried basil, crushed

¼ teaspoon salt

¼ teaspoon pepper

In a medium saucepan cook zucchini, onion, yellow pepper, and red pepper in hot oil for 5 to 8 minutes or till just tender. Transfer mixture to a medium mixing bowl. Stir in chopped tomato, olives, basil, salt, and pepper. Cover and chill for 4 to 24 hours.

⁂

Let salad stand at room temperature about 30 minutes before serving. Makes 4 to 6 servings.

ORIENTAL-STYLE VEGGIE SALAD

Ginger, toasted sesame oil, and garlic give these familiar vegetables an exotic nutty taste.

1 cup cauliflower flowerets

1 6-ounce package frozen pea pods

1 medium sweet red or yellow pepper, cut into bite-size strips

½ cup sliced water chestnuts, drained

2 tablespoons sliced green onion (2 medium)

Sesame Dressing

1 to 2 teaspoons sesame seed, toasted (optional)

In a covered saucepan cook cauliflower in boiling water for 2 minutes. Add pea pods and cook about 2 minutes more or till crisp-tender. Drain. In a mixing bowl combine cauliflower, pea pods, sweet pepper strips, water chestnuts, and green onion. Cover and chill for 4 to 24 hours.

To serve, shake Sesame Dressing well; pour over salad. Toss lightly to coat. Sprinkle with toasted sesame seed, if desired. Makes 4 servings.

SESAME DRESSING

In a screw-top jar combine 2 tablespoons *rice vinegar or white wine vinegar*, 2 tablespoons *salad oil*, 1 teaspoon grated *gingerroot*, 1 teaspoon *toasted sesame oil*, and 1 clove *garlic*, minced. Cover and shake well. Makes about ⅓ cup.

Toasted Sesame Oil

For salad dressings with a wonderfully nutty flavor, add a touch of toasted sesame oil. Look for this aromatic, reddish brown oil in Oriental food stores or specialty food sections of supermarkets. Because of its strong flavor, use toasted sesame oil only a teaspoon or two at a time. Don't use it as a salad oil or cooking oil. Also, don't confuse it with its untoasted cousin, labeled simply *sesame oil.* This light-colored oil has a mild flavor and may be used as a salad oil or cooking oil. It is sold in grocery and health food stores.

Time

Preparation	15 min.
Chilling	4 to 24 hrs.

Per Serving

Calories	116
Protein	2 g
Carbohydrate	9 g
Total Fat	8 g
Saturated Fat	1 g
Cholesterol	0 mg
Sodium	8 mg
Potassium	256 mg

Crunchy jicama, fresh cilantro, and ground red pepper give this slaw a Mexican twist.

JICAMA-CILANTRO SLAW

3 cups shredded cabbage with carrot

1 pound jicama, peeled and cut into thin strips (about 2 cups)

2 tablespoons sliced green onion (2 medium)

¼ cup salad oil

¼ cup lime juice

2 tablespoons snipped fresh cilantro or parsley

1 tablespoon sugar

¼ teaspoon salt

⅛ teaspoon ground red pepper

Fresh cilantro (optional)

Time

Preparation	15 min.
Chilling	2 to 24 hrs.

Per Serving

Calories	119
Protein	2 g
Carbohydrate	9 g
Total Fat	9 g
Saturated Fat	1 g
Cholesterol	0 mg
Sodium	100 mg
Potassium	188 mg

In a large mixing bowl combine shredded cabbage with carrot, jicama, and green onion.

For dressing, in a screw-top jar combine salad oil, lime juice, cilantro or parsley, sugar, salt, and red pepper. Cover and shake well. Pour the dressing over the cabbage mixture. Toss lightly to coat. Cover and chill for 2 to 24 hours.

To serve, toss slaw lightly. Garnish with cilantro, if desired. Makes 6 servings.

JULIENNE VEGETABLE SALAD

1½ cups water

1 medium zucchini, cut into julienne strips

2 stalks celery, cut into julienne strips

2 medium carrots, cut into julienne strips

1 sweet red or green pepper, cut into julienne strips

2 tablespoons sliced green onion (2 medium)

½ cup mayonnaise or salad dressing

¼ cup grated Parmesan cheese

2 teaspoons Dijon-style mustard

¼ teaspoon garlic powder

In a medium saucepan combine water, zucchini, celery, carrots, red or green pepper, and green onion. Cover and bring to boiling. Reduce heat; simmer about 3 minutes or till vegetables are just crisp-tender. Drain vegetables. Transfer to a large mixing bowl; set aside.

❧

For dressing, in a small mixing bowl stir together mayonnaise or salad dressing, Parmesan cheese, mustard, and garlic powder. Pour dressing over cooked vegetable mixture. Toss lightly to coat. Cover and chill for 4 to 24 hours. Makes 6 to 8 servings.

For this salad and other cooked vegetable salads, be sure to cook the vegetables just till tender. Overcooked vegetables lack texture and fall apart when mixed with the other ingredients.

Time

Preparation	30 min.
Chilling	4 to 24 hrs.

Per Serving

Calories	171
Protein	3 g
Carbohydrate	6 g
Total Fat	16 g
Saturated Fat	3 g
Cholesterol	14 mg
Sodium	240 mg
Potassium	237 mg

Salad Dressings

The crowning touch of any salad is a delectable dressing. Just the right one can turn a ho-hum bowl of ingredients into a harmonious composition. The recipes that follow include some new and unique salad dressings, as well as a variety of tried-and-true favorites—any of which will put your salads on the best-dressed list.

Herb Vinegar
(see recipe, page 218)

Fruit-Flavored Vinegar
(see recipe, page 218)

Low-Calorie Green Onion Dressing
(see recipe, page 214)

Orange-Poppy Seed Oil-Free Dressing
(see recipe, page 213)

Low-Calorie Tomato-Basil Vinaigrette
(see recipe, page 214)

MAYONNAISE

¼ teaspoon dry mustard

⅛ teaspoon salt

⅛ teaspoon paprika

Dash ground red pepper

1 egg yolk

2 tablespoons lemon juice

1 cup salad oil

In a small mixing bowl combine mustard, salt, paprika, and red pepper. Add egg yolk and lemon juice. Beat with an electric mixer on medium speed till combined. With mixer running, add oil, 1 teaspoon at a time, till 2 tablespoons have been added. Add the remaining oil in a thin, steady stream, beating constantly. This should take about 3 minutes (mixture should be thick). Cover and store in the refrigerator for up to 1 week. Makes about 1 cup (sixteen 1-tablespoon servings).

Time

Start to finish   10 min.

Per Serving

Calories	125
Protein	0 g
Carbohydrate	0 g
Total Fat	14 g
Saturated Fat	2 g
Cholesterol	13 mg
Sodium	17 mg
Potassium	5 mg

THOUSAND ISLAND DRESSING

1 cup mayonnaise or salad dressing

¼ cup chili sauce

2 tablespoons finely chopped pimiento-stuffed olives

2 tablespoons finely chopped green or sweet red pepper

2 tablespoons finely chopped onion

1 teaspoon Worcestershire sauce or prepared horseradish (optional)

1 hard-cooked egg, finely chopped

1 to 2 tablespoons milk (optional)

In a small mixing bowl combine mayonnaise or salad dressing and chili sauce. Stir in olives, green or sweet red pepper, onion, Worcestershire sauce or horseradish (if desired), and chopped egg. Cover and store in the refrigerator for up to 1 week. Before serving, if necessary, stir in milk to make the dressing the desired consistency. Makes 1½ cups (twenty-four 1-tablespoon servings).

Time

Start to finish   30 min.

Per Serving

Calories	73
Protein	0 g
Carbohydrate	1 g
Total Fat	8 g
Saturated Fat	1 g
Cholesterol	14 mg
Sodium	101 mg
Potassium	19 mg

CREAMY ITALIAN DRESSING

Time

Start to finish   10 min.

Per Serving

Calories	82
Protein	0 g
Carbohydrate	1 g
Total Fat	9 g
Saturated Fat	2 g
Cholesterol	8 mg
Sodium	77 mg
Potassium	11 mg

Same as Creamy Italian
Dressing except:
Calories	83
Sodium	78 mg
Potassium	12 mg

¾ cup mayonnaise **or** *salad dressing*

¼ cup dairy sour cream

2 teaspoons white wine vinegar **or** *white vinegar*

¼ teaspoon dry mustard

¼ teaspoon dried basil, crushed

¼ teaspoon dried oregano, crushed

⅛ teaspoon salt

⅛ teaspoon garlic powder

1 to 2 tablespoons milk (optional)

In a small mixing bowl stir together mayonnaise or salad dressing, sour cream, vinegar, mustard, basil, oregano, salt, and garlic powder. Cover and store in the refrigerator for up to 2 weeks. Before serving, if necessary, stir in milk to make the dressing the desired consistency. Makes about 1 cup (sixteen 1-tablespoon servings).

CREAMY GARLIC DRESSING

Prepare as above, *except* omit oregano and garlic powder. Add 2 cloves *garlic,* minced.

DIJON DRESSING

Time

Start to finish   10 min.

Per Serving

Calories	25
Protein	1 g
Carbohydrate	1 g
Total Fat	2 g
Saturated Fat	1 g
Cholesterol	5 mg
Sodium	46 mg
Potassium	23 mg

1 8-ounce carton dairy sour cream

½ cup milk

2 tablespoons Dijon-style mustard

1 tablespoon snipped parsley

2 teaspoons snipped fresh dill **or** *½ teaspoon dried dillweed*

In a small mixing bowl combine sour cream, milk, mustard, parsley, and dill. Cover and store in the refrigerator up to 1 week. Makes about 1½ cups (twenty-four 1-tablespoon servings).

GREEN GODDESS DRESSING

¾ cup packed parsley leaves

⅓ cup mayonnaise or salad dressing

⅓ cup dairy sour cream or plain yogurt

1 green onion, cut up

1 tablespoon vinegar

1 teaspoon anchovy paste or 1 anchovy fillet, cut up

¼ teaspoon dried basil, crushed

⅛ teaspoon garlic powder

⅛ teaspoon dried tarragon, crushed

1 to 2 tablespoons milk

In a blender container or food processor bowl combine parsley, mayonnaise, sour cream, onion, vinegar, anchovy paste, basil, garlic powder, and tarragon. Cover and blend or process till smooth. Cover and store in the refrigerator for up to 2 weeks. Before serving, stir in milk to make the dressing the desired consistency. Makes about 1 cup (sixteen 1-tablespoon servings).

Time

Start to finish   10 min.

Per Serving

Calories	45
Protein	0 g
Carbohydrate	1 g
Total Fat	5 g
Saturated Fat	1 g
Cholesterol	5 mg
Sodium	39 mg
Potassium	30 mg

BUTTERMILK-HERB DRESSING

½ cup mayonnaise or salad dressing

¼ cup dairy sour cream

2 tablespoons buttermilk

1 tablespoon snipped fresh basil or 1 teaspoon dried basil, crushed

1 tablespoon snipped parsley

¼ teaspoon pepper

¼ teaspoon garlic powder

¼ teaspoon onion powder

In a small mixing bowl stir together mayonnaise or salad dressing, sour cream, buttermilk, basil, parsley, pepper, garlic powder, and onion powder. Cover and store in the refrigerator for up to 1 week. Makes about 1 cup (sixteen 1-tablespoon servings).

Time

Start to finish   10 min.

Per Serving

Calories	58
Protein	0 g
Carbohydrate	1 g
Total Fat	6 g
Saturated Fat	1 g
Cholesterol	6 mg
Sodium	43 mg
Potassium	16 mg

Time

| Start to finish | 10 min. |

BLUE CHEESE DRESSING

Per Serving

Calories	41
Protein	2 g
Carbohydrate	1 g
Total Fat	4 g
Saturated Fat	1 g
Cholesterol	6 mg
Sodium	90 mg
Potassium	27 mg

½ cup plain yogurt **or** *dairy sour cream*

¼ cup cream-style cottage cheese

¼ cup mayonnaise **or** *salad dressing*

¾ cup crumbled blue cheese

2 to 3 tablespoons milk (optional)

In a blender container or food processor bowl combine yogurt or sour cream, cottage cheese, mayonnaise or salad dressing, and *¼ cup* of the blue cheese. Cover and blend or process till smooth. Stir in remaining blue cheese. If necessary, stir in milk to make the dressing the desired consistency. Cover and store in the refrigerator for up to 2 weeks. Makes about 1¼ cups (twenty 1-tablespoon servings).

Time

| Start to finish | 10 min. |

CREAMY HERB DRESSING

Per Serving

Calories	61
Protein	1 g
Carbohydrate	1 g
Total Fat	6 g
Saturated Fat	2 g
Cholesterol	6 mg
Sodium	74 mg
Potassium	26 mg

¼ cup loosely packed parsley leaves, fresh basil leaves, **or** *fresh tarragon leaves*

¼ cup mayonnaise **or** *salad dressing*

¼ cup dairy sour cream

2 tablespoons thinly sliced green onion (2 medium)

2 teaspoons lemon juice

2 teaspoons Dijon-style mustard

In a blender container or food processor bowl combine parsley, basil, or tarragon; mayonnaise or salad dressing; sour cream; green onion; lemon juice; and mustard. Cover and blend or process till smooth. Cover and store in the refrigerator for up to 1 week. Makes about ⅔ cup (nine 1-tablespoon servings).

CREAMY CUCUMBER SALAD DRESSING

Time

Start to finish   10 min.

½ cup mayonnaise **or** salad dressing

½ cup dairy sour cream

2 tablespoons snipped fresh chives **or** thinly sliced green onion

¾ cup peeled, seeded, and finely chopped cucumber (1 small)

2 tablespoons to ¼ cup milk

Per Serving

Calories	45
Protein	0 g
Carbohydrate	1 g
Total Fat	5 g
Saturated Fat	1 g
Cholesterol	5 mg
Sodium	30 mg
Potassium	18 mg

In a small mixing bowl stir together mayonnaise or salad dressing, sour cream, and chives or green onion. Stir in the chopped cucumber. Stir in milk to make the dressing the desired consistency. Cover and store in the refrigerator for up to 1 week. Makes about 1½ cups (twenty-four 1-tablespoon servings).

WALNUT VINAIGRETTE

Time

Start to finish   10 min.

½ cup walnut oil

⅓ cup white wine vinegar

2 tablespoons water

1 tablespoon sugar

1 tablespoon snipped fresh chives

1 tablespoon Dijon-style mustard

¼ teaspoon pepper

Per Serving

Calories	66
Protein	0 g
Carbohydrate	1 g
Total Fat	7 g
Saturated Fat	1 g
Cholesterol	0 mg
Sodium	31 mg
Potassium	4 mg

In a screw-top jar combine walnut oil, vinegar, water, sugar, chives, mustard, and pepper. Cover and shake well. Store in the refrigerator for up to 2 weeks. Shake well before serving. Makes about 1 cup (sixteen 1-tablespoon servings).

Time

Start to finish   10 min.

CRANBERRY-MINT VINAIGRETTE

Per Serving

Calories	56
Protein	0 g
Carbohydrate	4 g
Total Fat	5 g
Saturated Fat	1 g
Cholesterol	0 mg
Sodium	1 mg
Potassium	13 mg

½ cup cranberry juice cocktail

2 tablespoons salad oil

2 tablespoons vinegar

1 tablespoon snipped fresh mint **or** *½ teaspoon dried mint, crushed*

1 teaspoon sugar

In a screw-top jar combine cranberry juice cocktail, oil, vinegar, mint, and sugar. Cover and shake well. Store in the refrigerator for up to 3 weeks. Shake well before serving. Makes about ¾ cup (twelve 1-tablespoon servings).

Time

Start to finish   10 min.

SUN-DRIED-TOMATO VINAIGRETTE

Per Serving

Calories	37
Protein	1 g
Carbohydrate	3 g
Total Fat	3 g
Saturated Fat	0 g
Cholesterol	0 mg
Sodium	48 mg
Potassium	91 mg

¼ cup vinegar

¼ cup snipped sun-dried tomatoes (oil pack)

2 tablespoons oil from sun-dried tomatoes **or** *olive oil*

2 tablespoons water

1 tablespoon snipped fresh oregano **or** *tarragon*

or *1 teaspoon dried oregano* **or** *tarragon, crushed*

1 tablespoon Dijon-style mustard

1 teaspoon sugar

In a screw-top jar combine vinegar, snipped tomatoes, oil, water, oregano or tarragon, mustard, and sugar. Cover and shake well. Store in the refrigerator for up to 1 week. Shake well before serving. Makes about ¾ cup (twelve 1-tablespoon servings).

Basic Vinaigrette

⅓ cup salad oil

⅓ cup white wine vinegar or vinegar

1 tablespoon sugar (optional)

2 teaspoons snipped fresh thyme, oregano, or basil

or ½ teaspoon dried thyme, oregano, or basil, crushed

½ teaspoon paprika

¼ teaspoon dry mustard or 1 teaspoon Dijon-style mustard (optional)

In a screw-top jar combine oil, vinegar, sugar (if desired), desired herb, paprika, mustard (if desired), and ⅛ teaspoon *pepper*. Cover and shake well. Store in the refrigerator for up to 2 weeks. Shake well before serving. Makes about ¾ cup (twelve 1-tablespoon servings).

Red Wine Vinaigrette

Prepare as above, *except* reduce vinegar to *3 tablespoons*. Use *half* thyme and *half* oregano for the herb. Add 2 tablespoons *dry red wine* and 1 clove *garlic,* minced.

Italian Vinaigrette

Prepare as above, *except* use oregano for the herb and use the mustard. Add 2 tablespoons grated *Parmesan cheese,* ¼ teaspoon *celery seed,* and 1 clove *garlic,* minced.

Garlic Vinaigrette

Prepare as above, *except* omit herb and paprika. Add 2 large cloves *garlic,* minced.

Citrus and Poppy Seed Vinaigrette

Prepare as above, *except* substitute *lemon juice or lime juice* for the vinegar and *honey* for the sugar. Omit herb. Add 1 teaspoon *poppy seed.*

Ginger Vinaigrette

Prepare as above, *except* omit herb and mustard. Add 1 teaspoon grated *gingerroot.*

Time

Start to finish	10 min.

Per Serving

Calories	86
Protein	0 g
Carbohydrate	1 g
Total Fat	9 g
Saturated Fat	1 g
Cholesterol	0 mg
Sodium	2 mg
Potassium	8 mg

Same as Basic Vinaigrette except:

Calories	88
Potassium	10 mg

Same as Basic Vinaigrette except:

Calories	91
Carbohydrate	2 g
Cholesterol	1 mg
Sodium	18 mg
Potassium	13 mg

Same as Basic Vinaigrette except:

Carbohydrate	2 g

Same as Basic Vinaigrette except:

Calories	89
Carbohydrate	2 g
Sodium	0 mg
Potassium	14 mg

Same as Basic Vinaigrette except:

Potassium	10 mg

Healthy Salads

You may think that salads, because they contain lots of fruits and vegetables, are naturally healthy—that is, low in fat and calories—but that's not always true. Some salads are inherently high in fat and calories because they feature oily or creamy dressings or other rich ingredients such as avocados or olives. However, with a little planning, you easily can work salads into a healthy life-style. Here are a few helpful hints.

To control the amount of fat in your diet, plan your meals for the entire day, balancing occasional high-fat foods with low-fat ones. The amount of fat in any one food or recipe isn't as important as the total amount of fat you consume throughout the day.

When selecting salad recipes from this book, refer to the nutrition analysis that appears with each recipe. If you choose a main-dish salad that's high in fat, serve it with low-fat foods, such as a yeast bread (watch the margarine or butter) or low-fat crackers. Serve a high-fat side-dish salad with a lean entrée such as broiled orange roughy or grilled chicken breasts.

If you're looking for ways to lower your fat intake in general, here are some simple alterations you can make:

• If a salad calls for a homemade oil- or mayonnaise-based dressing, switch to one of the no-fat or low-calorie salad dressings on pages 213–215.

• If you opt for bottled salad dressing, your best bet is one that is fat-free. Reduced-calorie dressings are lower in fat than regular dressings, but many still contain significant amounts of fat. Check the nutrition information on the label before purchasing a reduced-calorie dressing.

• For a recipe that calls for mayonnaise or salad dressing, choose one of the commercial fat-free products.

• Limit the amounts of high-fat ingredients, such as avocados, olives, nuts, sausage, and cheeses, that you use in salads.

• For main-dish salads, take advantage of lean meats, poultry, fish, and reduced-fat cheeses.

OIL-FREE DRESSING

1 tablespoon powdered fruit pectin

¾ teaspoon snipped fresh **or** *¼ teaspoon dried oregano, basil,*
thyme, tarragon, savory, **or** *dillweed, crushed*

½ teaspoon sugar

⅛ teaspoon dry mustard

⅛ teaspoon pepper

¼ cup water

1 tablespoon vinegar

1 small clove garlic, minced

In a small mixing bowl stir together pectin, desired herb, sugar, dry mustard, and pepper. Stir in water, vinegar, and garlic. Cover and store in the refrigerator for up to 3 days. Makes about ½ cup (eight 1-tablespoon servings).

CREAMY ONION OIL-FREE DRESSING

Prepare as above, *except* increase sugar to *1 tablespoon*. Stir in ¼ cup sliced *green onion* and ¼ cup *plain yogurt* with the water. Makes about ¾ cup (twelve 1-tablespoon servings).

ORANGE-POPPY SEED OIL-FREE DRESSING

¼ teaspoon finely shredded orange peel

⅓ cup orange juice

1 tablespoon powdered fruit pectin

1 tablespoon honey

¼ teaspoon poppy seed

In a small mixing bowl stir together orange peel, orange juice, pectin, honey, and poppy seed. Cover and refrigerate for several hours or overnight before using. Cover and store in the refrigerator for up to 3 days. Makes about ½ cup (eight 1-tablespoon servings).

Time

Start to finish	*10 min.*

Per Serving

Calories	7
Protein	0 g
Carbohydrate	2 g
Total Fat	0 g
Saturated Fat	0 g
Cholesterol	0 mg
Sodium	0 mg
Potassium	5 mg

Same as Oil-Free Dressing except:

Calories	12
Carbohydrate	3 g
Sodium	4 mg
Potassium	20 mg

Time

Preparation	*10 min.*
Chilling	*3 to 8 hrs.*

Per Serving

Calories	18
Protein	0 g
Carbohydrate	5 g
Total Fat	0 g
Saturated Fat	0 g
Cholesterol	0 mg
Sodium	0 mg
Potassium	23 mg

Time

Start to finish   10 min.

Per Serving

Calories	5
Protein	0 g
Carbohydrate	1 g
Total Fat	0 g
Saturated Fat	0 g
Cholesterol	0 mg
Sodium	65 mg
Potassium	44 mg

LOW-CALORIE TOMATO-BASIL VINAIGRETTE

⅔ cup tomato sauce

¼ cup red wine vinegar

2 tablespoons snipped fresh basil **or** *1 teaspoon dried basil, crushed*

1 tablespoon water

1 teaspoon sugar

½ teaspoon Worcestershire sauce

¼ teaspoon prepared horseradish

In a screw-top jar combine tomato sauce, red wine vinegar, basil, water, sugar, Worcestershire sauce, and horseradish. Cover and shake well. Store in the refrigerator for up to 1 week. Shake well before serving. Makes about 1 cup (sixteen 1-tablespoon servings).

Time

Start to finish   10 min.

Per Serving

Calories	20
Protein	1 g
Carbohydrate	2 g
Total Fat	1 g
Saturated Fat	0 g
Cholesterol	2 mg
Sodium	51 mg
Potassium	35 mg

LOW-CALORIE GREEN ONION DRESSING

½ cup coarsely chopped green onion (8 medium)

¼ cup reduced-calorie mayonnaise **or** *salad dressing*

1 tablespoon white wine vinegar **or** *white vinegar*

1 tablespoon Dijon-style mustard

¼ teaspoon pepper

1 clove garlic, halved

1 8-ounce carton plain low-fat yogurt

In a blender container or food processor bowl combine green onion, mayonnaise or salad dressing, vinegar, mustard, pepper, and garlic. Cover and blend or process till onion is finely chopped. Transfer dressing to a mixing bowl. Stir in yogurt. Cover and store in the refrigerator for up to 1 week. Makes about 1¼ cups (twenty 1-tablespoon servings).

LOW-CALORIE THOUSAND ISLAND DRESSING

This low-cal version of Thousand Island dressing saves you 55 calories and 7 grams of fat per tablespoon over the version on page 205.

⅓ cup plain low-fat yogurt

2 tablespoons reduced-calorie mayonnaise or salad dressing

2 tablespoons chili sauce

1 tablespoon finely chopped green or sweet red pepper

1 tablespoon finely chopped onion

1 tablespoon skim milk

½ teaspoon paprika

1 hard-cooked egg white, finely chopped (optional)

In a small mixing bowl stir together the yogurt, mayonnaise or salad dressing, and chili sauce. Stir in the chopped green or sweet red pepper, onion, milk, paprika, and, if desired, the chopped egg white. Cover and store in the refrigerator for up to 1 week. Makes about ¾ cup (twelve 1-tablespoon servings).

Time

Start to finish   10 min.

Per Serving

Calories	18
Protein	1 g
Carbohydrate	2 g
Total Fat	1 g
Saturated Fat	0 g
Cholesterol	1 mg
Sodium	64 mg
Potassium	36 mg

215

Time

Preparation	*25 min.*
Standing	*1 wk.*

Per Serving

Calories	*120*
Protein	*0 g*
Carbohydrate	*0 g*
Total Fat	*14 g*
Saturated Fat	*2 g*
Cholesterol	*0 mg*
Sodium	*0 mg*
Potassium	*0 mg*

NUT-FLAVORED OIL

1½ cups unblanched, shelled, whole almonds, hazelnuts, **or** *walnuts (about 7½ ounces)*

2½ cups salad oil

Place nuts in a blender container or food processor bowl. Cover and blend or process till chopped. With blender or processor on slow speed, gradually add ½ *cup* of the oil through the opening in the lid. Blend or process till nuts are finely chopped.

❦

Transfer nut mixture to a small saucepan. Clip a candy or deep-fat cooking thermometer onto the side of the pan. Cook over low heat, stirring often, till thermometer registers 160°. Remove from heat and cool slightly. Combine the nut mixture with the remaining salad oil. Transfer to a 1-quart jar or bottle. Cover tightly and let stand in a cool place for 1 to 2 weeks.

❦

Line a colander with several layers of 100% cotton cheesecloth. Pour the oil mixture through the colander and let it drain into a bowl. Discard the nut paste. Transfer the strained liquid to a 1½-pint jar or bottle. If desired, add a few whole nuts to the jar or bottle. Cover the jar or bottle tightly. Store the oil in the refrigerator for up to 3 months. Makes about 2 cups (thirty-two 1-tablespoon servings).

Oil Options

No matter what kind of salad dressing you're preparing—a creamy mayonnaise or a sophisticated vinaigrette—it's important to select an oil that will enhance both the flavor of the dressing and the salad. Team mild-flavored oils with mild greens such as Boston, Bibb, sorrel, or oak-leaf lettuce. Strong oils go best with hearty greens such as arugula, mesclun, and radicchio.

Types

Salad oil or vegetable oil: Usually made from corn, soybeans, sunflowers, or peanuts, this oil is light yellow in color and rather bland in flavor.

Olive oil: Olive oil is made from pressed olives. You can buy different grades of olive oil. "Extra virgin" oil meets the highest standards and has a full-bodied, rich aroma and flavor. "Virgin" oil has slightly lower standards and is milder in flavor. "Pure" oil is made by blending lower quality olive oils with "extra virgin" or "virgin" olive oil. Even within these broad categories, differences in color and flavor exist. Green to greenish gold olive oil, pressed from green, semiripe olives, tastes slightly sharp. Golden olive oil, pressed from ripe olives, is more delicately flavored.

Sesame oil: There are two types of sesame oil. One, a thick, brown oil, is made from toasted sesame seed. It has a concentrated flavor and is used in very small amounts. (In our recipes, we refer to this type as "toasted sesame oil.") The other type of sesame seed oil is pale yellow and is made from untoasted sesame seed. It has a very mild sesame flavor. The two oils should not be used interchangeably.

Nut oil: Nut oils include walnut oil, hazelnut oil, and almond oil. Walnut and hazelnut oils are golden-colored with pronounced nut flavors and rich aromas. Almond oil is a clear, pale oil with a delicately sweet flavor. These oils usually are used in small amounts.

Storing

Except for nut oils, which always should be refrigerated, store oils at room temperature for 6 to 9 months (olive oil should be stored only for 6 months). If you want to chill olive oil, keep it in the refrigerator for up to 1 year. (When olive oil is chilled, it gets too thick to pour, so let it stand at room temperature for a few minutes or run warm water over the bottle before using it.)

HERB VINEGAR

Time

Preparation	10 min.
Standing	2 wks.

Per Serving

Calories	2
Protein	0 g
Carbohydrate	1 g
Total Fat	0 g
Saturated Fat	0 g
Cholesterol	0 mg
Sodium	5 mg
Potassium	15 mg

½ cup tightly packed fresh tarragon, thyme, mint, rosemary, or basil leaves

2 cups white wine vinegar

Wash desired herbs; pat dry with paper towels. In a small stainless steel or enamel saucepan combine herbs and vinegar. Bring *almost* to boiling. Remove from heat and cover loosely with cheesecloth; cool. Pour mixture into a clean 1-quart jar. Cover the jar tightly with a nonmetallic lid (*or* cover the jar with plastic wrap and then tightly seal with a metal lid). Let stand in a cool, dark place for 2 weeks.

❦

Line a colander with several layers of 100% cotton cheesecloth. Pour vinegar mixture through the colander and let it drain into a bowl. Discard herbs. Transfer strained vinegar to a clean 1½-pint jar or bottle. If desired, add an additional sprig of fresh herb to the jar. Cover jar with a nonmetallic lid (*or* cover with plastic wrap and tightly seal with a metal lid). Store in a cool, dark place up to 6 months. Makes about 2 cups (thirty-two 1-tablespoon servings).

FRUIT-FLAVORED VINEGAR

Time

Preparation	10 min.
Standing	2 wks.

Per Serving

Calories	6
Protein	0 g
Carbohydrate	1 g
Total Fat	0 g
Saturated Fat	0 g
Cholesterol	0 mg
Sodium	7 mg
Potassium	21 mg

1 cup fresh or frozen unsweetened tart red cherries, blueberries, or raspberries

2 cups white wine vinegar

Thaw fruit, if frozen. In a small stainless steel or enamel saucepan combine fruit and vinegar. Bring to boiling; reduce heat. Boil gently, uncovered, for 3 minutes. Remove from heat and cover loosely with cheesecloth; cool. Pour mixture into a clean 1-quart jar. Cover jar tightly with a nonmetallic lid (*or* cover with plastic wrap and then tightly seal with a metal lid). Let stand in a cool, dark place for 2 weeks.

❦

Line a colander with several layers of 100% cotton cheesecloth. Strain vinegar mixture through the colander and let it drain into a bowl. Discard fruit. Transfer strained vinegar to a clean 1-pint jar or bottle. If desired, add a few additional pieces of fresh fruit to the jar or bottle. Cover the jar or bottle tightly with a nonmetallic lid (*or* cover with plastic wrap and then seal tightly with a metal lid). Store vinegar in a cool, dark place for up to 6 months. Makes about 1½ cups (twenty-four 1-tablespoon servings).

Flavored Vinegars

Plain vinegar has long been a staple in the kitchen where it has been used mostly for canning and making pickles. But not anymore. Vinegars now come in many varieties, strengths, colors, and flavors, and can add pizzazz to salad dressings, sauces, soups, fish, and vegetables *without* adding extra sodium or fat. To help you decide which ones you'll enjoy, here's a quick rundown of the most common kinds.

Types

Balsamic: This dark brown vinegar, made from the juice of a very sweet grape, has a delicate, sweet flavor. Balsamic vinegar is aged in wooden barrels for at least 10 years, making it more expensive than other types.

Cider: A golden brown vinegar made from the juice of apples. It has a strong bite and faint apple flavor.

Fruit: Fruit vinegars are made with cider vinegar or white wine vinegar and any of a variety of fruits such as raspberries, strawberries, lemons, blueberries, or cranberries.

Herb: Herb vinegars are cider, white, or wine vinegars that have the added flavor of herbs. Herb vinegars can be made with basil, tarragon, oregano, thyme, mint, rosemary, dill, chervil, or garlic.

Rice: Used frequently in Oriental cooking, rice vinegars are made from rice wine or sake. Rice vinegars are usually clear to pale gold in color, and have a subtle tang and slightly sweet taste.

White or Distilled: This colorless vinegar is made from grain alcohol. It is the strongest and sharpest flavored of all vinegars.

Wine: These vinegars are made from fermented white, red, or rosé wine, champagne, or sherry. The color and flavor of these vinegars depend on the type of wine used. Red wine vinegar, for example, is more full-bodied than white wine vinegar.

Storing

Because it's so acidic, vinegar can be stored almost indefinitely at room temperature. Over time, you may notice some changes in color or the development of a sediment, but these changes don't affect the flavor.

Salad Accents

Herbed Wheat Bread
(see recipe, page 223)

Cheesy Cornmeal Batter Rolls
(see recipe, page 224)

Green Chili and Corn Muffins
(see recipe, page 227)

Easy-on-the-Cook Focaccia
(see recipe, page 230)

Onion and Garlic Breadsticks
(see recipe, page 225)

Brown-and-Serve Rye Rosettes
(see recipe, right)

Giant Pepperoni-Parmesan Muffins
(see recipe, page 228)

Beer-and-Onion Pull-Apart Loaves
(see recipe, page 222)

The cool crispness of a salad seems to call out for freshly baked bread. But who has time to make bread? Well, you do. In the time it takes to preheat your oven, you can mix up these muffins or popovers. Or, with a little planning, you can pull together our make-ahead yeast breads that rise overnight in the refrigerator. Match any of these mouth-watering homemade breads with a main-dish salad and you've got a complete meal.

BROWN-AND-SERVE RYE ROSETTES

2¾ to 3¼ cups all-purpose flour

1 package active dry yeast

½ cup milk

½ cup plain yogurt

¼ cup honey

¼ cup margarine **or** butter

½ teaspoon salt

2 eggs

1 cup rye flour

1 tablespoon caraway seed

With brown-and-serve rolls (rolls that are partially baked and then frozen) you can have hot yeast bread at a moment's notice.

In a large mixing bowl combine *1½ cups* of the all-purpose flour and yeast; set aside. In a medium saucepan combine milk, yogurt, honey, margarine or butter, and salt. Heat and stir *just till warm* (120° to 130°) and margarine almost melts. Add to flour mixture. Add eggs. Beat with an electric mixer on low to medium speed for 30 seconds, scraping the sides of the bowl. Beat on high speed for 3 minutes. Using a wooden spoon, stir in the rye flour, caraway seed, and as much of the remaining all-purpose flour as you can.

⚜

Turn dough out onto a lightly floured surface. Knead in enough of the remaining all-purpose flour to make a moderately stiff dough that is smooth and elastic (6 to 8 minutes total). Shape into a ball. Place in a greased bowl; turn once. Cover and let rise in a warm place till double (about 1 hour).

⚜

Punch dough down. Turn out onto a lightly floured surface. Divide dough in half. Cover and let rest 10 minutes. Divide each half into 12 pieces. Roll each piece into a 12-inch rope. Tie each rope in a loose knot, leaving 2 long ends. Tuck one end under the knot. Bring the other end up and tuck it into the top center of the knot. Place rolls 2 to 3 inches apart on greased baking sheets. Cover and let rise in a warm place till *nearly* double (about 30 minutes).

⚜

Bake in a 325° oven for 10 minutes; *do not brown.* Remove from baking sheets and cool on wire racks. Wrap in moisture- and vaporproof wrap. Seal, label, and freeze.

⚜

To serve, remove wrap. Thaw rolls at room temperature for 10 to 15 minutes. Bake on ungreased baking sheets in a 375° oven for 10 to 12 minutes or till golden. Makes 24.

Time

Preparation	25 min.
Rising	1½ hrs.
Shaping	20 min.
Baking	20 min.
Thawing	10 min.

Per Serving

Calories	109
Protein	3 g
Carbohydrate	18 g
Total Fat	3 g
Saturated Fat	1 g
Cholesterol	19 mg
Sodium	78 mg
Potassium	66 mg

221

These savory loaves make serving a cinch because they break apart into individual rolls.

BEER-AND-ONION PULL-APART LOAVES

3 tablespoons margarine or butter

1 cup finely chopped onion (2 medium)

1 teaspoon sugar

4½ to 5 cups all-purpose flour

1 package active dry yeast

1 12-ounce can (1½ cups) beer

2 tablespoons sugar

½ teaspoon salt

1 tablespoon margarine or butter, melted

In a small saucepan melt the 3 tablespoons margarine or butter. Add onion and the 1 teaspoon sugar. Cook and stir till onion is tender but not brown.

⋇

In a large mixing bowl combine *1½ cups* of the all-purpose flour and yeast; set aside. In a medium saucepan combine beer, the 2 tablespoons sugar, and salt. Heat and stir *just till warm* (120° to 130°). Add to flour mixture. Beat with an electric mixer on low to medium speed for 30 seconds, scraping the sides of the bowl. Beat on high speed for 3 minutes. Using a wooden spoon, stir in the onion mixture and as much of the remaining flour as you can.

⋇

Turn dough out onto a lightly floured surface. Knead in enough of the remaining flour to make a moderately stiff dough that is smooth and elastic (6 to 8 minutes total). Cover and let rest 10 minutes.

⋇

Divide dough into 16 pieces; shape each piece into a ball. Place *eight* balls in each of *two* greased 8x4x2-inch loaf pans. Cover loosely with plastic wrap. Refrigerate for 2 to 24 hours.

⋇

To bake, remove plastic wrap. Let loaves stand at room temperature for 20 minutes. Puncture any air bubbles with a greased wooden toothpick. Brush with the 1 tablespoon melted margarine or butter. Bake in a 375° oven for 35 to 40 minutes or till golden. (If necessary, cover with foil the last 10 minutes of baking to prevent overbrowning.) Remove from pans and cool on wire racks. Makes 2 loaves (16 servings).

Time

Preparation	45 min.
Chilling	2 to 24 hrs.
Standing	20 min.
Baking	35 min.

Per Serving

Calories	167
Protein	4 g
Carbohydrate	28 g
Total Fat	4 g
Saturated Fat	1 g
Cholesterol	0 mg
Sodium	111 mg
Potassium	65 mg

HERBED WHEAT BREAD

Try basil in place of the chervil in this hearty round loaf.

1¼ to 1¾ cups all-purpose flour

1 package active dry yeast

¾ cup milk

1 tablespoon sugar

½ teaspoon salt

1 egg

1 cup whole wheat flour

¼ cup toasted wheat germ

1 tablespoon snipped fresh chervil **or** *1 teaspoon dried chervil, crushed*

1 tablespoon snipped fresh thyme **or** *½ teaspoon dried thyme, crushed*

In a large mixing bowl combine *1 cup* of the all-purpose flour and yeast; set aside. In a small saucepan combine milk, sugar, and salt. Heat and stir *just till warm* (120° to 130°). Add to flour mixture. Add egg. Beat with an electric mixer on low speed for 30 seconds, scraping the sides of the bowl. Beat on high speed for 3 minutes. Using a wooden spoon, stir in whole wheat flour, wheat germ, chervil, thyme, and as much of the remaining all-purpose flour as you can.

❧

Turn dough out onto a lightly floured surface. Knead in enough of the remaining flour to make a moderately stiff dough that is smooth and elastic (6 to 8 minutes total). Shape dough into a ball. Place in a greased 1½-quart soufflé dish or casserole; turn once to grease the surface. With a sharp knife, cut a 4-inch cross, ½ inch deep, in the top of the loaf. Cover loosely with plastic wrap. Refrigerate for 2 to 24 hours.

❧

To bake, remove plastic wrap. Let the loaf stand at room temperature for 20 minutes. Puncture any air bubbles with a greased wooden toothpick. Bake in a 350° oven for 30 to 35 minutes or till golden. Remove from dish. Cool on a wire rack. Makes 1 loaf (16 servings).

Time

Preparation	30 min.
Chilling	2 to 24 hrs.
Standing	20 min.
Baking	30 min.

Per Serving

Calories	76
Protein	3 g
Carbohydrate	14 g
Total Fat	1 g
Saturated Fat	0 g
Cholesterol	14 mg
Sodium	77 mg
Potassium	89 mg

Place any leftover rolls in a freezer bag or container and freeze them for up to 3 months. To serve, thaw the rolls at room temperature for 1 hour or wrap them in foil and heat them in a 300° oven about 20 minutes.

Time

Preparation	20 min.
Rising	30 to 45 min.
Baking	15 min.

Per Serving

Calories	124
Protein	4 g
Carbohydrate	17 g
Total Fat	4 g
Saturated Fat	2 g
Cholesterol	20 mg
Sodium	124 mg
Potassium	62 mg

CHEESY CORNMEAL BATTER ROLLS

2 cups all-purpose flour

1 package active dry yeast

1 tablespoon snipped fresh oregano **or** *1 teaspoon dried oregano, crushed*

1 cup milk

¼ cup sugar

2 tablespoons margarine **or** *butter*

½ teaspoon salt

1 egg

1 cup shredded cheddar cheese (4 ounces)

½ cup yellow cornmeal

Grease eighteen 2½-inch muffin cups; set aside. In a large mixing bowl combine *1 cup* of the flour, yeast, and oregano; set aside.

❧

In a small saucepan combine milk, sugar, margarine or butter, and salt. Heat and stir *just till warm* (120° to 130°) and margarine almost melts. Add to flour mixture. Add egg. Beat with an electric mixer on low to medium speed for 30 seconds, scraping the sides of the bowl. Beat on high speed for 3 minutes. Using a wooden spoon, stir in the remaining flour, the cheese, and cornmeal (batter will be sticky).

❧

Spoon batter into prepared muffin cups. Cover and let rise in a warm place till *nearly* double (30 to 45 minutes).

❧

Bake in a 375° oven for 15 to 20 minutes or till golden brown. Cool in pans for 10 minutes. Remove from pans and cool completely on wire racks. Makes 18.

ONION AND GARLIC BREADSTICKS

2¼ to 2¾ cups all-purpose flour

1 package active dry yeast

¼ cup finely chopped onion

2 cloves garlic, minced

2 tablespoons salad oil

¾ cup milk

1 tablespoon sugar

½ teaspoon salt

1 egg white

1 tablespoon water

2 tablespoons grated Parmesan cheese (optional)

Bake enough breadsticks to serve with dinner tonight and freeze the rest for another meal.

In a large mixing bowl combine *¾ cup* of the flour and yeast; set aside. In a small saucepan cook onion and garlic in hot oil till onion is tender but not brown. Add milk, sugar, and salt. Heat *just till warm* (120° to 130°). Add milk mixture to flour mixture. Beat with an electric mixer on low to medium speed for 30 seconds, scraping the sides of the bowl. Beat on high speed for 3 minutes. Using a wooden spoon, stir in as much of the remaining flour as you can.

꙰

Turn dough out onto a lightly floured surface. Knead in enough of the remaining flour to make a stiff dough that is smooth and elastic (8 to 10 minutes total). Cover; let rest 10 minutes.

꙰

Divide dough into 24 pieces. Roll each piece into an 8-inch-long rope. Place 1 inch apart on greased baking sheets. Cover and let rise in a warm place till *nearly* double (15 to 20 minutes).

꙰

In a small mixing bowl stir together egg white and water. Brush breadsticks with egg white mixture. Sprinkle with Parmesan cheese, if desired. Bake in a 375° oven for 10 to 12 minutes or till golden. Remove from baking sheets. Cool on wire racks. Makes 24.

FREEZER BREADSTICKS

Prepare as above, *except* after shaping the dough, cover the baking sheets loosely with plastic wrap; freeze till firm. Transfer breadsticks to a moisture- and vaporproof plastic bag; seal and label. Freeze up to 4 weeks. To bake, remove breadsticks from freezer; place 1 inch apart on greased baking sheets. Cover and let stand at room temperature for 1 hour. Brush with egg white mixture and, if desired, sprinkle with Parmesan cheese. Bake as directed above.

Time

Preparation	45 min.
Rising	15 to 20 min.
Baking	10 min.

Per Serving

Calories	48
Protein	1 g
Carbohydrate	7 g
Total Fat	1 g
Saturated Fat	0 g
Cholesterol	1 mg
Sodium	51 mg
Potassium	38 mg

Fill these crispy, hollow puffs with a creamy, tossed, main-dish salad such as Beef Salad with Fresh Basil Dressing *(see recipe, page 63).*

BASIL AND GARLIC POPOVERS

1 tablespoon shortening **or** *nonstick spray coating*

2 beaten eggs

1 cup milk

1 tablespoon salad oil

1 clove garlic, minced

1 cup all-purpose flour

1 tablespoon snipped fresh basil **or** *½ teaspoon dried basil, crushed*

¼ teaspoon salt

Using *½ teaspoon* of shortening for *each* cup, grease the bottoms and sides of six 6-ounce custard cups or the cups of a popover pan. *Or,* spray cups with nonstick coating. Place the custard cups on a 15x10x1-inch baking pan; set aside.

In a medium mixing bowl combine eggs, milk, salad oil, and garlic. Using a wire whisk or a rotary beater beat egg mixture till combined. Add flour, basil, and salt. Beat till smooth. Fill the prepared cups *half* full of batter. Bake in a 400° oven about 40 minutes or till very firm and crusts are golden brown.

Immediately after removing popovers from the oven, prick each popover with a fork to let the steam escape. Turn off the oven. For crisper popovers, return the popovers to the oven for 5 to 10 minutes or till desired crispness is reached. Remove popovers from cups and serve immediately. Makes 6.

Time

Preparation	15 min.
Baking	40 min.

Per Serving

Calories	161
Protein	6 g
Carbohydrate	18 g
Total Fat	7 g
Saturated Fat	2 g
Cholesterol	75 mg
Sodium	132 mg
Potassium	112 mg

Green Chili and Corn Muffins

1 cup all-purpose flour

1 cup yellow cornmeal

2 to 4 tablespoons sugar

1 tablespoon baking powder

¼ teaspoon salt

2 beaten eggs

1 cup milk

¼ cup salad oil **or** *shortening, melted*

1 12-ounce can whole kernel corn with sweet peppers **or** *whole kernel corn, drained*

2 tablespoons chopped green chili peppers

Grease eighteen 2½-inch muffin cups. Set aside.

✣

In a large mixing bowl stir together flour, cornmeal, sugar, baking powder, and salt. Make a well in the center of the dry ingredients.

✣

In a medium mixing bowl combine eggs, milk, and oil or melted shortening. Add the egg mixture all at once to the dry ingredients. Stir *just till moistened* (batter should be lumpy). Fold in corn and chili peppers.

✣

Spoon batter into the prepared muffin cups, filling each ⅔ full. Bake in a 400° oven about 20 minutes or till edges are golden. Cool in muffin cups for 5 minutes. Remove from muffin cups. Serve warm. Makes 18.

This recipe makes a basketful of muffins. If there are too many to eat at one meal, wrap the leftovers in heavy foil and freeze them for up to 3 months. To serve, heat the wrapped, frozen muffins in a 350° oven for 15 to 18 minutes.

Time

Preparation	15 min.
Baking	20 min.

Per Serving

Calories	116
Protein	3 g
Carbohydrate	17 g
Total Fat	4 g
Saturated Fat	1 g
Cholesterol	25 mg
Sodium	162 mg
Potassium	87 mg

To make smaller muffins, grease twelve 2½-inch muffin cups or line them with paper bake cups. Fill each ⅔ full with batter. Bake in a 400° oven for 20 to 25 minutes.

GIANT PEPPERONI-PARMESAN MUFFINS

1½ cups all-purpose flour

¼ cup grated Parmesan cheese

2 tablespoons sugar

2 teaspoons baking powder

⅛ teaspoon salt

1 beaten egg

¾ cup milk

¼ cup salad oil

⅓ cup chopped pepperoni

1 tablespoon grated Parmesan cheese

Time

Preparation	15 min.
Baking	25 min.

Per Serving

Calories	305
Protein	9 g
Carbohydrate	30 g
Total Fat	16 g
Saturated Fat	4 g
Cholesterol	45 mg
Sodium	439 mg
Potassium	130 mg

Grease six 3½-inch muffin cups or six 6-ounce custard cups. *Or,* line muffin cups or custard cups with paper bake cups. Set aside.

In a medium mixing bowl combine flour, the ¼ cup Parmesan cheese, sugar, baking powder, and salt. Make a well in the center of the dry ingredients.

In another medium mixing bowl combine egg, milk, and salad oil. Add the egg mixture all at once to the dry ingredients. Stir *just till moistened* (batter should be lumpy). Fold in the chopped pepperoni.

Spoon batter into the prepared muffin cups, filling each ⅔ full. Sprinkle the 1 tablespoon Parmesan cheese on top of the batter.

Bake in a 375° oven for 25 to 30 minutes or till a toothpick inserted near the center of a muffin comes out clean. Remove muffins from muffin cups or custard cups; cool slightly on a wire rack. Serve warm. Makes 6.

Giant Pepperoni-
Parmesan Muffins
(see recipe, left)

Herbed Wheat Bread
(see recipe, page 223)

Onion and Garlic
Breadsticks
(see recipe, page 225)

Green Chili and
Corn Muffins
(see recipe, page 227)

Brown-and-Serve
Rye Rosettes
(see recipe, page 221)

Baguette Croutons
(see recipe, page 231)

Focaccia (foh COT see uh) is an Italian yeast bread, similar to deep-dish pizza crust, with a breadlike texture. This easy-on-the-cook version starts with refrigerated breadsticks.

Time

Preparation	15 min.
Baking	12 min.

Per Serving

Calories	246
Protein	7 g
Carbohydrate	36 g
Total Fat	8 g
Saturated Fat	1 g
Cholesterol	2 mg
Sodium	508 mg
Potassium	60 mg

EASY-ON-THE-COOK FOCACCIA

1 package (8) refrigerated breadsticks

¼ cup chopped onion

2 teaspoons snipped fresh rosemary **or** *basil* **or** *½ teaspoon dried rosmeary* **or** *basil, crushed*

1 tablespoon olive oil **or** *salad oil*

2 tablespoons grated Parmesan cheese

Separate the breadsticks into 8 pieces, leaving them coiled. Place the coils 3 inches apart on a lightly greased baking sheet. Press each coil into a 4-inch circle.

❦

In a small skillet cook onion and rosemary or basil in hot oil till onion is tender but not brown. Spoon some of the onion mixture over each coil. Sprinkle each with Parmesan cheese.

❦

Bake in a 375° oven about 12 minutes or till golden. Remove from baking sheet. Cool slightly on a wire rack. Serve warm. Makes 4 servings.

Parmesan Croutons

Time

Preparation	*10 min.*
Baking	*15 min.*

¼ cup margarine or butter

3 tablespoons grated Parmesan cheese

⅛ teaspoon garlic powder

4 ½-inch-thick slices French bread, cut into ¾-inch cubes

Per Serving

Calories	*55*
Protein	*1 g*
Carbohydrate	*5 g*
Total Fat	*3 g*
Saturated Fat	*1 g*
Cholesterol	*1 mg*
Sodium	*102 mg*
Potassium	*11 mg*

In a large skillet melt margarine or butter. Remove from heat. Stir in Parmesan cheese and garlic powder. Add bread cubes, stirring until cubes are coated with margarine mixture.

❦

Spread bread cubes in a single layer in a shallow baking pan. Bake in a 300° oven for 10 minutes; stir. Continue baking about 5 minutes more or till bread cubes are dry and crisp. Cool completely before using.

❦

Store tightly covered for up to 1 week. Transfer to a serving bowl and serve as a salad accompaniment. Makes about 2 cups (sixteen 2-tablespoon servings).

Italian Croutons

Prepare as above, *except* stir ½ teaspoon *Italian seasoning,* crushed, into the margarine or butter mixture.

Same as Parmesan Croutons

Dill Croutons

Prepare as above, *except* omit the garlic powder and the Parmesan cheese. Stir 1 teaspoon dried *dillweed* into the melted margarine or butter.

Same as Parmesan Croutons except:
Calories	*51*
Carbohydrate	*4 g*
Cholesterol	*0 mg*
Sodium	*84 mg*

Baguette Croutons

Cut 20 to 24 slices, about ¼ inch thick, from a loaf of *French or Italian bread.* Prepare the margarine mixture as directed above. Brush the margarine mixture on *one* side of *each* bread slice. Place slices in a single layer in a shallow baking pan. Bake in a 300° oven for 10 to 15 minutes or till dry and crisp. Makes 20 to 24 croutons (10 to 12 servings).

Same as Parmesan Croutons except:
Calories	*98*
Protein	*2 g*
Carbohydrate	*9 g*
Total Fat	*6 g*
Sodium	*183 mg*
Potassium	*22 mg*

231

Buying Guide

Most of our recipes call for cup measures of greens, which sometimes makes it difficult to know how much to buy. Our handy chart should make it easier. Refer to it when planning your grocery list.

Greens	Weight as Purchased	Unit Before Preparation	Measure After Preparation
Arugula	1 ounce		1½ cups torn
Belgian endive	4 ounces	1 head	20 leaves
Bok choy	1¼ pounds	1 head	7 cups coarsely chopped
Butterhead lettuce (Boston or Bibb)	¾ pound	1 head	4 cups torn
Cabbage	2 pounds	1 head	12 cups shredded
Chinese cabbage	2 pounds	1 head	10 cups coarsely chopped
Collard greens	½ pound		4 cups torn
Curly endive	¾ pound	1 head	10 cups torn
Dandelion greens	½ pound		6 cups torn
Escarole	½ pound	1 head	7 cups torn
Iceberg lettuce	1¼ pounds	1 head	10 cups torn 12 cups shredded
Kale	½ pound		7 cups torn
Leaf lettuce	¾ pound	1 head	8 cups torn
Mustard greens	½ pound		12 cups torn
Radicchio	½ pound	1 head	5½ cups torn
Romaine	1 pound	1 head	6 cups torn
Sorrel	1 ounce		1 cup torn
Spinach	1 pound		12 cups torn, stems removed
Watercress	¼ pound		2⅓ cups, stems removed

Index

Nutrition Analysis

Keep track of your daily nutrition needs by using the information we provide at the end of each recipe. We've analyzed the nutrition content of each recipe serving for you. When a recipe gives an ingredient substitution, we used the first choice in the analysis. If it makes a range of servings (such as 4 to 6), we used the smallest number. Ingredients listed as optional weren't included in the calculations.

Index

Z

Tips

Recipe Time Estimates

The timings listed with each recipe should be used only as general guidelines. Some cooks will work faster and others will work slower than the times given. Here are some other points to remember when referring to these timings:

● Preparation timings have been rounded to the nearest 5-minute increment.

● Listings include the time to chop, slice, or otherwise prepare ingredients (such as cooking rice, when a recipe calls for cooked rice).

● When a recipe gives an ingredient substitution (1 cup sliced kiwi fruit or halved strawberries), calculations were made using the first ingredient.

● When a recipe gives alternate cooking methods (such as broiling or grilling directions), timings refer to the first method.

● Timings assume some steps can be performed simultaneously. For example, vegetables may be cut up while the water for cooking pasta comes to a boil.

● The preparation of optional ingredients is not included.

Metric Conversions

Metric Cooking Hints

By making a few conversions, cooks in Australia, Canada, and the United Kingdom can use the recipes in Better Homes and Gardens® *Salads* with confidence. The charts on this page provide a guide for converting measurements from the U.S. customary system, which is used throughout this book, to the imperial and metric systems. There also is a conversion table for oven temperatures to accommodate the differences in oven calibrations.

Volume and Weight: Americans traditionally use *cup* measures for liquid and solid ingredients. The chart (top right) shows the approximate imperial and metric equivalents.
If you are accustomed to weighing solid ingredients, here are some helpful approximate equivalents:
- 1 cup butter, caster sugar, or rice = 8 ounces = about 250 grams
- 1 cup flour = 4 ounces = about 125 grams
- 1 cup icing sugar = 5 ounces = about 150 grams

Spoon measures are used for smaller amounts of ingredients. Although the size of the teaspoon is the same, the size of the tablespoon varies slightly among countries. However, for practical purposes and for recipes in this book, a straight substitution is all that's necessary.

Measurements made using cups or spoons always should be *level,* unless stated otherwise.

Product Differences: Most of the ingredients called for in the recipes in this book are available in English-speaking countries. However, some are known by different names. Here are some common American ingredients and their possible counterparts:
- Sugar is granulated or caster sugar.
- Powdered sugar is icing sugar.
- All-purpose flour is plain household flour or white flour. When self-rising flour is used in place of all-purpose flour in a recipe that calls for leavening, omit the leavening (baking soda or baking powder) and salt.
- Light corn syrup is golden syrup.
- Cornstarch is cornflour.
- Baking soda is bicarbonate of soda.
- Vanilla is vanilla essence.

Useful Equivalents

⅛ teaspoon = 0.5ml	⅔ cup = 5 fluid ounces = 150ml
¼ teaspoon = 1ml	¾ cup = 6 fluid ounces = 175ml
½ teaspoon = 2ml	1 cup = 8 fluid ounces = 250ml
1 teaspoon = 5ml	2 cups = 1 pint
¼ cup = 2 fluid ounces = 50ml	2 pints = 1 litre
⅓ cup = 3 fluid ounces = 75ml	½ inch = 1 centimetre
½ cup = 4 fluid ounces = 125ml	1 inch = 2 centimetres

Baking Pan Sizes

American	Metric
8x1½-inch round baking pan	20x4-centimetre sandwich or cake tin
9x1½-inch round baking pan	23x3.5-centimetre sandwich or cake tin
11x7x1½-inch baking pan	28x18x4-centimetre baking pan
13x9x2-inch baking pan	32.5x23x5-centimetre baking pan
12x7½x2-inch baking dish	30x19x5-centimetre baking pan
15x10x2-inch baking pan	38x25.5x2.5-centimetre baking pan (Swiss roll tin)
9-inch pie plate	22x4- or 23x4-centimetre pie plate
7- or 8-inch springform pan	18- or 20-centimetre springform or loose-bottom cake tin
9x5x3-inch loaf pan	23x13x6-centimetre or 2-pound narrow loaf pan or pâté tin
1½-quart casserole	1.5-litre casserole
2-quart casserole	2-litre casserole

Oven Temperature Equivalents

Fahrenheit Setting	Celsius Setting*	Gas Setting
300°F	150°C	Gas Mark 2
325°F	160°C	Gas Mark 3
350°F	180°C	Gas Mark 4
375°F	190°C	Gas Mark 5
400°F	200°C	Gas Mark 6
425°F	220°C	Gas Mark 7
450°F	230°C	Gas Mark 8
Broil		Grill (watch time and heat)

Electric and gas ovens may be calibrated using Celsius. However, increase the Celsius setting 10 to 20 degrees when cooking above 160°C with an electric oven. For convection or forced-air ovens (gas or electric), lower the temperature setting 10°C when cooking at all heat levels.